בַּחַנְפֵי לַעֲגֵי מָעוֹג חָרֹק עָלַי שִׁנֵּימוֹ:

אֲדֹנָי כַּמָּה תִּרְאֶה הָשִׁיבָה נַפְשִׁי מִשֹּׁאֵיהֶם מִכְּפִירִים יְחִידָתִי:

אוֹדְךָ בְּקָהָל רָב בְּעַם עָצוּם אֲהַלְלֶךָּ:

אַל־יִשְׂמְחוּ־לִי אֹיְבַי שֶׁקֶר שֹׂנְאַי חִנָּם יִקְרְצוּ־עָיִן:

כִּי לֹא שָׁלוֹם יְדַבֵּרוּ וְעַל רִגְעֵי־אֶרֶץ דִּבְרֵי מִרְמוֹת יַחֲשֹׁבוּן:

וַיַּרְחִיבוּ עָלַי פִּיהֶם אָמְרוּ הֶאָח הֶאָח רָאֲתָה עֵינֵינוּ:

רָאִיתָה יְהוָה אַל־תֶּחֱרַשׁ אֲדֹנָי אַל־תִּרְחַק מִמֶּנִּי:

הָעִירָה וְהָקִיצָה לְמִשְׁפָּטִי אֱלֹהַי וַאדֹנָי לְרִיבִי:

שָׁפְטֵנִי כְצִדְקְךָ יְהוָה אֱלֹהָי וְאַל־יִשְׂמְחוּ־לִי:

אַל־יֹאמְרוּ בְלִבָּם הֶאָח נַפְשֵׁנוּ אַל־יֹאמְרוּ בִּלַּעֲנוּהוּ:

יֵבֹשׁוּ וְיַחְפְּרוּ יַחְדָּו שְׂמֵחֵי רָעָתִי

יִלְבְּשׁוּ־בֹשֶׁת וּכְלִמָּה הַמַּגְדִּילִים עָלָי:

יָרֹנּוּ וְיִשְׂמְחוּ חֲפֵצֵי צִדְקִי וְיֹאמְרוּ תָמִיד

יִגְדַּל יְהוָה הֶחָפֵץ שְׁלוֹם עַבְדּוֹ:

וּלְשׁוֹנִי תֶּהְגֶּה צִדְקֶךָ כָּל־הַיּוֹם תְּהִלָּתֶךָ:

לַמְנַצֵּחַ לְעֶבֶד־יְהוָה לְדָוִד:

נְאֻם־פֶּשַׁע לָרָשָׁע בְּקֶרֶב לִבִּי

אֵין־פַּחַד אֱלֹהִים לְנֶגֶד עֵינָיו:

כִּי־הֶחֱלִיק אֵלָיו בְּעֵינָיו לִמְצֹא עֲוֹנוֹ לִשְׂנֹא:

דִּבְרֵי־פִיו אָוֶן וּמִרְמָה חָדַל לְהַשְׂכִּיל לְהֵיטִיב: [יִמְאָס:

אָוֶן יַחְשֹׁב עַל־מִשְׁכָּבוֹ יִתְיַצֵּב עַל־דֶּרֶךְ לֹא־טוֹב רָע לֹא

טוֹב:

בְּגָרְשֵׁהוּ וַיֵּלַךְ :
...ל־דָּוִד בְּשַׁנּוֹתוֹ אֶת־טַעְמוֹ לִפְנֵי אֲבִימֶלֶךְ וַיְגָרְשֵׁ
אֲבָרֲכָה אֶת־יְהוָה בְּכָל־עֵת תָּמִיד תְּהִלָּתוֹ בְּפִי :
בַּיהוָה תִּתְהַלֵּל נַפְשִׁי יִשְׁמְעוּ עֲנָוִים וְיִשְׂמָחוּ :
... גַּדְּלוּ לַיהוָה אִתִּי וּנְרוֹמְמָה שְׁמוֹ יַחְדָּו :
דָּרַשְׁתִּי אֶת־יְהוָה וְעָנָנִי וּמִכָּל־מְגוּרוֹתַי הִצִּי...
הִבִּיטוּ אֵלָיו וְנָהָרוּ וּפְנֵיהֶם אַל־יֶחְפָּרוּ :
זֶה עָנִי קָרָא וַיהוָה שָׁמֵעַ וּמִכָּל־צָרוֹתָיו הוֹשִׁיעוֹ :
חֹנֶה מַלְאַךְ־יְהוָה סָבִיב לִירֵאָיו וַיְחַלְּצֵם :
טַעֲמוּ וּרְאוּ כִּי טוֹב יְהוָה ...רֵי הַגֶּבֶר יֶחֱסֶה
יְראוּ אֶת־יְהוָה ...שָׁיו כִּי אֵין מַחְסוֹר לִירֵאָיו :
כְּפִירִים רָשׁוּ וְרָעֵבוּ וְדֹרְשֵׁי יְהוָה לֹא־יַחְסְרוּ כָל־ט...
לְכוּ־בָנִים שִׁמְעוּ־לִי יִרְאַת יְהוָה אֲלַמֶּדְכֶם :
מִי־הָאִישׁ הֶחָפֵץ חַיִּים אֹהֵב יָמִים לִרְאוֹת ט...
נְצֹר לְשׁוֹנְךָ מֵרָע וּשְׂפָתֶיךָ מִדַּבֵּר מִרְמָה :
סוּר מֵרָע וַעֲשֵׂה־טוֹב בַּקֵּשׁ שָׁלוֹם וְרָדְפֵהוּ :
עֵינֵי יְהוָה אֶל־צַדִּיקִים וְאָזְנָיו אֶל־שַׁוְעָתָם :
פְּנֵי יְהוָה בְּעֹשֵׂי רָע לְהַכְרִית מֵאֶרֶץ זִכְרָם :
צָעֲקוּ וַיהוָה שָׁמֵעַ וּמִכָּל־צָרוֹתָם הִצִּילָם :
קָרוֹב יְהוָה לְנִשְׁבְּרֵי־לֵב וְאֶת־דַּכְּאֵי־רוּחַ יוֹשִׁיעַ :
רַבּוֹת רָעוֹת צַדִּיק וּמִכֻּלָּם יַצִּילֶנּוּ יְהוָה :
שֹׁמֵר כָּל־עַצְמוֹתָיו אַחַת מֵהֵנָּה לֹא נִשְׁבָּרָה :
תְּמוֹתֵת רָשָׁע רָעָה וְשֹׂנְאֵי צַדִּיק יֶאְשָׁמוּ :
פּוֹדֶה יְהוָה נֶפֶשׁ עֲבָדָיו וְלֹא יֶאְשְׁמוּ כָּל־הַחֹסִים בּוֹ :

H KITA

Poetry as Prayer
The Psalms

Poetry as Prayer
The Psalms

M. Basil Pennington, OCSO

Artwork by Helen Kita

Pauline
BOOKS & MEDIA
BOSTON

Library of Congress Cataloging-in-Publication Data

Pennington, M. Basil.
    Poetry as prayer : the Psalms / M. Basil Pennington.
        p. cm. — (The poetry as prayer series)
    Includes bibliographical references.
    ISBN 0-8198-5927-3
        1. Bible. O.T. Psalms—Meditations. I. Title. II. Series.

BS1430.54 .P46 2001
    223'.206—dc21

                                                    00-062332

Printed and published in the U.S.A. by Pauline Books & Media,
50 Saint Pauls Avenue, Boston MA 02130-3491.

www.pauline.org.

Pauline Books & Media is the publishing house of the Daughters
of St. Paul, an international congregation of women religious
serving the Church with the communications media.

1 2 3 4 5 6   06 05 04 03 02 01

This book is dedicated to
the Monks of Assumption Abbey
who pray the Psalms night and day
for all the human family.

Contents

———

Introduction

Enter King David.

We might imagine the strikingly handsome young king, crown on his head and harp in his hands, kneeling in the courts of the Lord, pouring out his heart in worship and praise. Or we might see him, clothes disheveled and torn, in the darkness of the royal chamber, a tearful face worn with anguish: "Have mercy on me, O Lord, have mercy." With poetic imagination, uniting ourselves with the inspired singer, our Psalm prayer finds new color and depth.

The historicity of such scenes may be questionable. While today's scholars are willing to admit the actual Davidic authorship, or at least an authorship contemporary with him, of a significant number of the Psalms—maybe as many as seventy-three; certainly 2, 16, 18, 29, 60, 68, 82, 108, and 110—some Psalms were clearly composed later. The authors, even when named, are for the most part lost to history. But because David features largely in the Psalms, tradition allows us to speak of him as the author of the collection. In any case, the divinely inspired poetry fulfills its purpose. For it is in poetic imagery that the Psalms speak to us and invite us into their experience.

In this new millennium, we are gratefully witnessing a growing awareness of the things of the Spirit. This includes a renewed interest in the Psalms, especially as a vehicle for prayer. This is most beneficial. Be they 2,500 years or more than 3,000 years old (as scholars are more and more accepting), in the Psalms we still find the emotions, desires, and fears that challenge us today. They tutor us in the divinely inspired way to respond to these realities in our lives, but we can be formed and informed by this means of divine guidance only if we allow ourselves to be fully open to the poetic experience the Psalmist wants to share with us.

Let us, then, take a look at the Psalms as poetry, and at the imaging of God that these inspired songs place before us. Together, let us experience a few of these beautiful and powerfully moving songs.

A practical note: The translations of the Scriptures in this volume are largely my own, though they are admittedly strongly influenced by those of others, most notably the *New Revised Standard Version*, the *Jerusalem Bible* and Rev. Mitchell Dahood's excellent work in the *Anchor Bible*.

M. Basil Pennington, OCSO
Assumption Abbey

Chapter 1

An Inspired Poetry

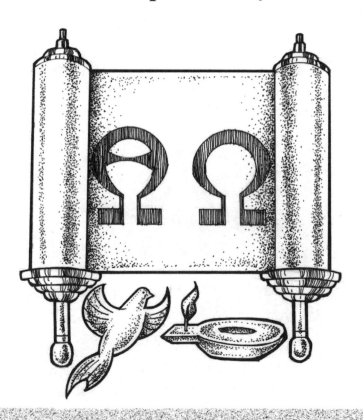

Prayer, like everything else, begins with God. God speaks, we respond.

In the beginning, God first spoke our wondrous creation into being. The stars…how often have we stood beneath them on a cold, crisp night and experienced our hearts reaching out *beyond* beyond. The words of the Psalmist serve us very well here:

Praise Yahweh from the heavens,
praise Yahweh from the heights.

Praise Yahweh, all you angels of Yahweh,
praise Yahweh, all you hosts of Yahweh.

Praise Yahweh, sun and moon,
praise Yahweh, all you stars.

Praise Yahweh, heaven of heavens….

(Ps 148:1–4)

The wonder of it! The Psalmist reminds us, "He knows each star by its name" (Ps 147:4).

And then there is the sea, vast and wide, with its creatures beyond all counting (Ps 104:25). And the hills and the deserts—the Psalms speak of them, calling us to experience not only their wonder, but also the wonder of their Maker who speaks to us through them. They are wondrous poetry, written in water and stone and all the stuff of creation.

The Imagery of Creation

The poetic images, even the ones drawn from nature, are fully pregnant for us only if we hear them in their overall Scriptural context. For example, the image of the eagle in Psalm 17:8: "Guard me as the apple of the eye; hide me in the shadow of your wings…," speaks to us more fully because of Deuteronomy 32:10: "He sustained him in a desert land, in a howling wilderness waste; he shielded him, cared for him, guarded him as the apple of his eye." And it is the image in Jeremiah 5:6: "Therefore a lion from the forest shall kill them, a wolf from the desert shall destroy them…" that concretizes and fleshes out the image of the wolf in the next verse of Psalm 17: "From the wicked who despoil me, my deadly enemies who surround me…," letting it have its full power.

The Creator of all these wonders, our God, did not stay afar off as One to be seen with awe. Our God came close and spoke to us through the Word, by means of human words that we can actually begin to understand, words that lead the mind to the heart, and through the heart to our transcendent God who dwells within.

But what our God wants to share with us, God's own self-revelation, is something far too great for human words alone, for mere conceptual knowledge. So God uses the story and the myth, the image and the analogy, the all embracing freedom of the poetic word.

Sacred Poetry

I sometimes wonder how many of those who pray the Psalms think of them as poems and approach them the way we must approach poetry for it to effect us as it is meant to. When God inspired the various writers who were to compose our sacred books, God inspired some to convey his message of wisdom and love in and through poetry. And we fully receive the message that God intended and that the inspired author sought to convey only if we open ourselves to the Psalms as poetry. What is revealed in the Psalter is revealed within poetic form and is only ours to the extent that we are able to enter the poetic experience of the author.

Generally, the poetic word not only conveys a concept, but also affections and spiritual associations which produce an experience that touches and enriches our depths as human persons. As we let poetry speak to us, we do not primarily seek to discern references to things outside the poem, except insofar as these references may be vehicles or instruments to help us enter into the unique experience the poem is offering us. For example, as we pray Psalm 51, we do not attend so much to David and the historical context of his sin as we do to our own bones being crushed, our own crushed and broken heart, our own need to be healed and washed clean.

It is this inner reality, the "soul" of the poem, that we hope will call us forth and enrich our lives. Sometimes one particular verse or phrase seems to catch or incarnate this "soul" for us. The first verse of Psalm 17, "Destroy deceitful lips," names the theme of the whole Psalm. At other times, the animating spirit is woven inexpressibly through the whole of the poem.

The Psalms are, indeed, a tremendously rich and beautiful collection of poems. Their cosmic symbolism covers an entire spectrum—from peaceful and beautiful pastoral scenes to the entire creation stirred to its very heights in a wild chaotic storm. In this natural symbolism, our tradition meets all the great religions of the world, for we share here a common heritage and experience. In these poems, those of differing beliefs can sing a common song with us. Here a primitive, perhaps natural revelation of

God is made to us all and prepares us for the more spiritual, personal Revelation that is ours in the Jewish covenant and ultimately in the Incarnation.

The natural, cosmic symbolism is exceedingly wondrous, soul-stirring and embracing. It invites us to constant prayer, for this cosmos is ever around us. It makes our lives more beautiful and hopeful as it transforms our experience and translates God's love-message into something we can more readily perceive. Frequent immersion in the Psalms is like living in a repeated embrace of the Divine Love.

Jesus and the Psalms

As Christians, we look to Jesus to teach us how to pray. In this, as in all, he teaches us more by example than by word. As a Jew, he certainly prayed the Psalms, as did all his People. But do we ever imagine Jesus reading poetry—learned at his father's knee, perhaps? Jesus reciting poetry—even on the cross? Singing it with his apostles at the first Eucharist? For the Psalms are indeed poems. A Rabbi told me that traditionally, devout Jews constantly recite the Psalms in order to make the Word become part of them, instantly available for application to life's circumstances. This certainly was Christ's own experience. The Psalms filled Jesus' life. They came spontaneously to his lips, even in the ultimate moments of his life. They formed his heart.

The Church and the Psalms

In this tradition, the Church makes the Psalms very much the fabric of its prayer in continuously praying these ancient poems. For Catholic Christians, the Eucharistic Celebration is the central act of all prayer, and rarely, if ever, do we celebrate it without some Psalm-poetry to help us enter into this great prayer. Then, too, the Psalms weave through the day in the portions of the Church's Liturgy of the Hours, creating the setting for the Eucharist in our daily lives. This weaving allows the grace and reality of the Eucharist to be continuously present to us. The Psalms have traditionally helped the faithful to raise minds and hearts to God, motivating us to give ourselves over to living completely the reality of who we are as men and women baptized into Christ, who share in the divine life of intimate love and communion.

Praying the Psalms aloud, as in the Liturgy of the Hours, is an incarnational way to pray, involving much more of the human person, giving the soul of the Word a greater opportunity to engrave itself within us. Certainly this is one of the values of a common recitation of the Psalms or of singing them together as did the Jews of old and of today, as did early Christian communities and monastic communities through the centuries, as do many parishes today. Another value of reciting these songs aloud or singing them is the time this provides for inviting the memory and imagination to clothe the concepts with their rich imagery and emotional associations.

The Psalms: Gateway to Contemplation

Recitation or chanting of the Psalms is not meant to be a sort of esoteric form of prayer, something used to try to induce psychological states of consciousness. Rather, the Psalms are meant to help us to understand and express who we are, both in hope and in reality. When we pray, all our words are little words, rooted in the *Word* who alone is the fullness of meaning. The Psalms' poetic words become ever more life-giving and creative to the extent that they are "inhabited" by the creative Spirit of the Word.

The poetic experience as an esthetical experience is not itself contemplation—at least not in the way we speak of contemplation as prayer: deep union and communion with God in love. Poetry can foster a kind of "acquired" contemplation, a contemplation of the wonders of reality such as beauty, might, splendor, goodness. Therefore, poetry can be the gateway to *true* contemplation. Cultivating the habit of "pondering" the Sacred Scriptures, carrying in our mind and heart certain verses—those that come to be especially meaningful to us through chanting or reading or listening to the Psalms—preserves within us the atmosphere necessary for true contemplation. It guards a certain "purity of heart." And it is the pure of heart—blessed are they—who will see God. The presence of the Sacred Text in our mind and heart can protect us from evil thoughts and feelings, from the movements of the passions, from all sorts of temptations, which find no room to take root within us when the Word of God is occupying the space. Rather, the sacred words invoke the Divine Presence and fill us with hope and joy. God's word makes God present. God's word becomes our word and speaking to God bonds us to God and God to us.

God's Spirit opens the poetic verses of the Psalms for us and we are brought into their deeper spiritual meanings. It is by the Spirit that we are led into true contemplation and to prayer in spirit and in truth. The rich poetic experience of the Psalms supports our abiding in the Word so that Holy Spirit can act within us and gently lead us into their most precious and life-giving depths.

The Psalms' poetic, rich imagery helps us to escape the narrow confines of an often all-too-customary self-centeredness. Enticed toward something more beautiful, more grand, more wondrous, we go beyond ourselves. In this new and larger space, the Spirit has room to operate, to lead us further into the depths of this perceived beauty and grandeur and into the Divine.

Praying as Christ's Body

As we listen to the Psalms and recite them in a spirit of faith and love, the Holy Spirit works mightily within us. At the same time, we fill out the meaning of the words with our *own* experiences of joy and sorrow, struggle and conflict, suffering and victory. Some days this is easier than others. One day we feel more in tune with the Psalms of praise. Another day, "out of the depths we cry." But if we are conscious of our oneness with the whole Christ, we know that each and every emotion belongs to us, not only in our oneness with the Saints in heaven, but with our sisters and brothers in all corners of the earth, living their many diverse conditions and situations. Our "Praise God" can make us one with the great choir in Saint Peter's, and our "Have mercy on us, Lord" rises with that of the oppressed in East Africa. The Psalms give piercing voice to our deepest distress and they leap with the joy of our brightest moments. And always, they can lead us into the serenity of a hope which knows that the darkest hours will pass, that passing joy is but an overture for the eternal joy that awaits us.

All of this is not just artistic expression. When we believe what our faith teaches us and open ourselves to the Holy Spirit, a transformation takes place within us. When we are open to the operation of the Spirit, even if a Psalm-poem does not seem to draw us into its experiential dimension, transformation can take place. We are immersed in the deepest waters that flow in silence far below the ups and downs of the poetic experience. At this level, we are experiencing our oneness with *Christ's being to the Father in the love who is Holy Spirit*. It is ever the Christ, the whole Christ, with whom we have been "oned," who is True Pray-er, the Poet, singing to the Father in, through, and with us. This poetic experience is Reality. And through the Psalms we have entered into this Reality.

The Psalms Tell Our Story

Besides providing this rich cosmic imagery, the Psalms recount in poetic form the great events of Salvation History as they were lived under the Sinaiatic Covenant. We Christians read them as a mystical prefiguring of the fulfilling events of the New Covenant, which are even now being carried out by the Holy Spirit in our own lives as we journey toward the eternal Kingdom, the true promised land. In the Psalms we are invited to get more profoundly in touch with who we are and to more profoundly live and experience our life in Christ who died on Calvary, rose, and now lives as Head of his members.

With our emphasis on the poetic character of the Psalms, we do not mean to downplay the importance of serious scholarly study of the Psalter. Many scholars and commentators undertake great efforts to determine the "literary form" of each Psalm: a wisdom Psalm, a Psalm of thanksgiving, an individual lament, a prayer for healing and so forth. And some of the Psalms seem to be actually two or more distinct poems that have been joined together, such as Psalm 40, which is both a hymn of thanksgiving and a lament.

Addressing this at the beginning of his commentary on Psalm 36, Father Mitchell Dahood writes: "The coexistence of three literary types within a poem of thirteen verses points out the limitations of the form-critical approach to the Psalter." For prayer, therefore, I think it best to approach each Psalm with great openness and to let it reveal itself to us and call us forth. As we grow in familiarity with the Psalms, we will begin to know which Psalm best suits us, as the particular circumstances of our life succeed one another.

Poetry is very personal. It communicates by evoking an experience from within. God uses the poetic experience of the Psalm to communicate to me. This and my response to it, form the communication that we call prayer. The Psalms give me not only God's communication to me, but also most apt words and sentiments, as well as excellent modeling, on how to respond. So excellent are these poems that Jesus, the Son of God himself, used them. United with Jesus as Pray-er, who is also the One about whom the Psalms are often speaking, we can offer to God a most perfect response when we pray the Psalms, remembering that the Psalms are poetry, only fully understood when understood and expressed as poems.

Chapter 2

Hebrew Poetry

What do people think of when they think of poetry? Perhaps a simple rhyme:

Now I lay me down to sleep.
I pray the Lord my soul to keep.
And if I die before I wake,
I pray the Lord my soul to take.

Perhaps rhythm, which is far more important and more intrinsic to the poetic genre, helping a particular poem to carry out its essential task of drawing the listener into the experience to be shared:

The moon is a ghostly galleon
Tossed upon cloudy seas.

Hebrew poetry, however, takes a different approach. Occasionally there might be rhyme in Hebrew poetry, but it is rare; it sometimes possesses a certain rhythm, for there is certainly rhythm (almost necessarily lost in translation) in the strophes of Psalm 5, which alternately contrast the "just" and the "wicked." Yet, neither rhyme nor rhythm is Hebrew poetry's main composites for accomplishing its integral communication.

Metaphor, image, and symbol—these are the main tools of Hebrew poetic craft. It is these that touch something deep within, calling forth our emotions and associations. It is these that give voice to what is deepest within us. It is these that are able to bear a burden of communication, a message far too dense for the merely conceptual. God and his ways are certainly beyond all our words and concepts: "My thoughts are not your thoughts, nor my ways your ways, says the Lord. But as high as heaven is above the earth, so are my thoughts beyond your thoughts and my ways beyond your ways" (Is 55:8). "Eye has not seen, nor ear heard, nor has it entered into the human mind what God has prepared for those who love God" (1 Cor 2:9). Metaphors, analogies, and stories can take us beyond the concept into the realm of experience and into an open space for Divine communication. And the Psalms are exceedingly rich in these.

I imagine every Christian at one time or another has wished that he or she could read and sing and pray the Psalms in Hebrew as Jesus did. Happily, many of our Jewish friends and even some of our Christian friends have come to make this language their own and can share with us something of the richness of their experience.

Hebrew Poetry's Secret

But even if we cannot understand Hebrew, Hebrew poetry contains an element that greatly helps us to enter the fullness of its experience. This characteristic of Hebrew poetry is its abundant, varied parallelism. A poetic line is followed by a line that in some way invites us to enter more deeply the experience being expressed, thus "paralleling" the first line.

In simple synonymous parallelism, the succeeding line expresses the same idea as the preceding line but in different words, adding colors and connotations that fill out and enrich what is conveyed:

For he spoke and it was,
he commanded and it stood forth.

(Ps 33:9)

How good to sing hymns to our God,
how satisfying it is to praise our Glorious One.

(Ps 147:1)

Or additional images might be used which enrich the poetic device:

He gathers the waters of the sea into a jar,
he puts the depths into storehouses.

(Ps 33:7)

In parallelism there is almost always some development of thought. Sometimes this is done by a certain movement from the abstract to the concrete:

How blessed is the nation Yahweh God has blessed,
the people he has chosen as his own patrimony.

(Ps 33:12)

Here the poet further describes the blessing the people received: to become the Chosen People, God's patrimony.

Parallelism includes cases where a common subject joins two parallel actions more intimately:

How can you lie in wait for my life,
and pursue me like a bird?

(Ps 11:1)

Sometimes it is a question of making a request more specific:

When I call answer me, O God of my vindication;
in my distress, set me free.

(Ps 4:2)

Sometimes there is a real development of the image within the parallel verses:

You will break them with a rod of iron,
shatter them like a potter's jar.

(Ps 2:9)

Or the parallel will support a request with an additional reason:

Make them perish, O God, let them fall because of their plotting;
for their many crimes throw them down.

(Ps 5:11)

More interestingly, parallelism sometimes allows an image to be enriched by opposites or an antithesis:

You are the Strong One who saves the poor,
you humble the eyes of the proud.

(Ps 18:28)

They were stooped over and fell down,
while we stood erect and self-assured.

(Ps 20:9)

To the orphan and the widow Yahweh gives confidence,
but the power of the wicked Yahweh undermines.

(Ps 146:9)

More complex patterns appear. Here we have a parallel pair within another parallel, called an inclusion:

I am praying to you, Yahweh;
at dawn hear my voice

> *at dawn I will draw up my case.*
> *For you will I watch.*

(Ps 5:3–4)

Sometimes a pair of parallels pile up more imagery on a preceding pair, almost overwhelming us with the abundance:

> *Rescue my neck from the sword,*
> *my face from the blade of the ax.*
> *Save me from the lion's jaws,*
> *from the horns of the wild oxen make me safe.*

(Ps 22:21–22)

And sometimes an antithesis is skillfully thrown in:

> *With the faithful you are faithful,*
> *with the honest you are honest.*
> *With the sincere you are sincere,*
> *but with the cunning you are cunning.*

(Ps 18:26–27)

And then there are triplets:

> *All who see me make fun of me.*
> *They gape at me.*
> *They wag their heads.*

(Ps 22:8)

A common subject often binds the images closely together:

Look, he conceives malice,
is pregnant with evil doing
and gives birth to treachery.

(Ps 7:15)

And these tightly bound images can be piled one atop another to paint an ever-fuller picture for us:

He who walks with integrity
and practices justice
and speaks the truth from his heart.
He who does not trip over his tongue,
who does no wrong to any other,
who detracts not from his neighbor's good name.

(Ps 15:1–2)

Repetition can add further power to the image we are invited to enter:

The voice of Yahweh is very strength,
the voice of Yahweh is majesty itself,
the voice of Yahweh shatters the cedars,
shatters the cedar of Lebanon.

(Ps 29:4–5)

Yahweh sets prisoners free,
Yahweh opens the eyes of the blind.
Yahweh straightens those bent double.

(Ps 146:8)

Sometimes the use of parallelism in the structure of a poem can be very intricate. For example, in the Hebrew, Psalm 29 has fourteen "beats" (or accentuated syllables) from the beginning of this Psalm to the verse "the appearance of the Holy One," and fourteen "beats" from the end of the Psalm to the parallel verse, "the vision of the Glorious One."

How wondrous this particular characteristic of Hebrew poetry, the parallel: it paints scenes in most vivid colors, fills them with sound and movement, calls forth emotions in abundance! And it is a characteristic with a staying power in translation. Whether using cosmic imagery or raw human emotions, Psalms speak to us immediately, call forth memories of our own experience, and catch us up into sharing the experience they seek to convey.

Translating Poetry

Over the years, I have traveled to many different parts of the world to lead people in the ancient Christian tradition of Centering Prayer. Often I have needed translators, who were never very happy when I quoted the old, Latin adage: *Traductor traditor est—The translator is a traitor.* No matter how good a translator may be, when we leave a word behind to embrace its literal equivalent in another language, we leave behind a whole rich collection of nuances and associations and take on another entire network of the same.

When it comes to poetry, if the translator uses rhyme, the rhyme scheme is obviously something belonging to the new expression quite exclusively. An exceptionally good translator can sometimes capture some of the original poem's rhythm and let that rhythm continue to exercise its ability to bring the listener or reader into the desired poetic experience. More common than either rhythm or rhyme are metaphors, allegories, and images from the original that find their way into the new linguistic effort. But these are valuable only if they continue to bring the listener into the same experience found in the original. This is the essence of the poetic genre: to bring one into an experience. Translation, then, is successful only to the extent that it provides the same experiential opportunity provided in the poem's original language.

There are many English translations of the Psalter available today—some better than others—and each succeeding version has benefited from a rich on-going scholarship. Nevertheless, when faced with a difficult passage even the best of scholars will at times admit that a "translation is problematic" and acknowledge that "this solution will be dispensed with when a better solution is proposed for this enigmatic verse."

It is a time of great fluidity in Psalm research. Whatever be their merits from a scholarly and literary point of view, each translation does reflect its own translator's subjective experience or lack of it. While we believe in a special inspirational grace accompanying the original authors and editors as they produced their texts, we can also hold that Divine Providence is able and willing to work through the final results of the translator's labors and textual product. We should not allow scholarly concerns to delay our entrance into *lectio* and prayer with the Psalter. We can confidently take up the inspired Word of God, the hymns and songs of the Psalter, and trust that God will speak to us through them. As we open ourselves to them, God will invite us to enter into a revealing experience.

CHAPTER 3

Psalm 1:
The Just and the Wicked

Psalm 1

How blest are they who
have not entered the council of the wicked,
nor stood in the assembly of sinners,
nor sat in the session of scoffers.
From the Law of the Lord is their delight;
from Yahweh's Law they recite day and night.

They are like trees transplanted near streams of
    water:
they yield their fruit in due season,
their leaves will never wither.
In all that they do, they prosper.

Not so the wicked:
these are like winnowed chaff
driven along by the wind.

The wicked shall not stand in the judgment
nor sinners in the gathering of the just.

Yahweh will keep the assembly of the just safe
while the assembly of the wicked shall perish.

Psalm 1 stands as the prologue in the *Book of Psalms.*
More than that, it actually summarizes the essential
wisdom teaching of the Psalms: Yahweh will keep the
just safe and they will prosper, while the wicked will find
themselves in Sheol, the place of darkness.

**How blest are they who
have not entered the council of the wicked,
nor stood in the assembly of sinners,
nor sat in the session of scoffers.**

In a way, the poet teaches us a lesson right from the
start: accentuate the positive, count your blessings, dwell
on what is good and not on what is bad or what is miss-
ing. However, he follows this almost immediately with
a negation in describing the blessed just ones. Why? The
poet has in mind here a common situation of his time.
A town or village was generally ruled by a council or
assembly of elders who sat in the town's gateway as they
discussed the inhabitants' affairs. It sometimes happened

that these elders were more concerned with preserving their shreds of authority and power than with the welfare of the town. This would be the sort of assembly Jezebel wrote to in order to have the just man Naboth stoned to death so that her husband could have his vineyard (cf. 1 Kings 21). The just would have no part of such an assembly. The just would not come before it seeking help, nor would they take a place within such a gathering.

However, these verses can be understood more broadly as referring to the wicked in general, to sinners and to scoffers, those who scoff at the Law, who have little regard for that to which God calls them, his Chosen People, through Revelation.

It is quite different with the just:

From the Law of the Lord is their delight;
from Yahweh's Law they recite day and night.

Structurally, the poem opens with a triplicate having a common subject, a very tight-knit and full parallelism. Then we move to a more ordinary and simple parallel, the second half of which indicates concretely how the first—taking delight—is expressed in the life of the just. In later Psalms, we will certainly hear a good bit more about the poet's delight in the Law.

The Ever-Present Word

For our Jewish sisters and brothers, the Law in some way is an incarnation, the concrete presence of God in the midst of his People, speaking to them. This is obvious in formal Jewish worship. But the everyday way devout Jews express their devotion is, first of all, by giving time to serious study of the sacred Word, pronouncing the words with their lips as they do so. This repetition carries over into their prayer where these same words express the aspirations of their hearts, and then into their conversation, where the Word guides, answers problems, raises questions, challenges all ungodliness. Ideally, this recitation of the Word will carry over into the rest of Jewish life, so that no matter what they are doing, their lips will meditate wisdom, quietly forming the sacred words. The Law is God's Word, God's Presence, and they never want to be separated from it.

For the first twelve centuries of the Christian era, this is how the faithful understood meditation. By reading or hearing the Sacred Word or a word from a spiritual mother or father, the devout would receive a "Word of Life." They would then seek to keep this word constantly with them, repeating it in their minds and even on their lips, until it entered deeply within to form their heart. Thus, they moved toward constant prayer and an ever-deeper union and communion with God through the Word of his Law.

The Life-Sustaining Word

In the Psalm's next verse, poetic imagery enters in:

They are like trees transplanted near streams of
    water:
they yield their fruit in due season,
their leaves will never wither.

In a land that always knew a scarcity of water, the rare stream was a striking sight, a verdant stretch of rich green. If one were fortunate enough to have such a treasured stream flowing through his property, he would plant his best fruit trees right beside it. For this fruit tree, he would never need to fear drought; he would never have to labor to irrigate them abundantly. They would have all the water ever needed.

Here, the poet invites us to see the Law, the Sacred Scriptures, the Psalms themselves, as such a stream. If we root ourselves near the Sacred Text, in the Law, and draw constantly from it, we will have very fruitful lives. Our faith, our hope will never wither. Some commentators see more here, with eternal life promised in the words "will never wither." This may be reading something into the text and into the mind of the poet, but it is nonetheless quite true. A life constantly watered by the wisdom of the Scriptures will surely lead to eternal life. And that is the whole sense of this introductory poem and of the Psalter as a whole.

Notice that the poet says that the just ones are "like trees transplanted." By God's grace and by using our God-given freedom, we have to be transplanted, we have to undergo a conversion from sin. To be among the just ones, we must root ourselves near God's holy Word and let all our life be watered by it.

These verses provide a simple parallel: "they yield fruit/their leaves never wither." The next lines are a parallel of contrast and they open the way for the poet to speak of the just one's opposite: the wicked.

The Wind-Blown Chaff

In all that they do, they prosper.
Not so the wicked:

With this simple introduction, the poet reaches for a suitable image for the wicked. He does not have to go far, using a sight common for him, although perhaps not as common for us.

These are like winnowed chaff
driven along by the wind.

This reminds me of a delightful and grace-filled visit I had some years ago to the Island of Patmos. My gracious friend Bishop Kallistos, a monk of the Orthodox monastery that crowns the Island, had offered me the use of his rooms there. From this commanding height, I could see the entire small island, a picture that had probably not changed much in centuries. Farmers worked their small fields and tended their rows of vines. Grapes lay on the roofs slowly becoming raisins. Donkeys wended their way around the threshing floors while husky workers tossed the grain in the air and the chaff went flying away, driven before the sea breezes.

Yes, the chaff was driven away. The poet may well have been thinking of the wicked being driven into Sheol, as he would say more explicitly in Psalm 35:

Let them be like chaff before the wind,
with the angel of Yahweh driving them.

Let them be sent into darkness and destruction
with the angel of Yahweh pursuing them.

If agrarian imagery does not speak to us city dwellers, I suspect we might easily enough imagine the gusts of autumn winds driving the leaves, sand, and litter of the gutters along our city streets.

Preparing for the finale, the poet returns to his beginning image of an assembly, though it is not exactly the same:

The wicked shall not stand in the judgment
nor sinners in the gathering of the just.

Again, the subject does not stand in the assembly where he has no place. There is a kind of inclusion here, as this verse links to the first verse of the Psalm. But a very different gathering is envisioned. In the first verse, it was a gathering in the gateway of the city. Here instead, it is the "gathering in" of all the just on the last day. Judgement will be meted out and the wicked will have no place here, no plea to enter, no opportunity to join the just.

Choosing Life

Again, as did the ever-green leaves of the just, something here hints at life beyond the grave, an eternal life or death. For this reason, there are two different translations of the very important final verse of this Psalm, both with good arguments for their different renderings of a particular Hebrew word. The translation I have chosen favors a hint of "something more," of the eternal assembly to which all this is to leading.

**Yahweh will keep the assembly of the just safe
while the assembly of the wicked shall perish.**

But one can also justify the other translation:

**Yahweh will keep the way of the just safe
while the way of the wicked shall perish.**

And indeed, of the two, this might be the more encouraging and consoling one for us who are still on the way.

The message of this opening Psalm, this prologue to the Psalter, is that there are two ways to walk on the journey, two paths: the way of the just and the way of the wicked. It all comes down to that. If we are wise and heed the wisdom of the Psalter, we will choose the way of the just. To find that way and to stay with it, we must keep close to the Law, the inspired Word of God.

CHAPTER 4

Psalm 19:
The Illumination of the Law

Psalm 19 [18]

The vault of the heavens proclaims the glory of God,
the sky itself manifests his hands' work
day pours forth its speech to day,
night shares its knowing with night
without speech and without words,
without their voice being heard.

Their cry goes forth through all the earth
and their words to the end of the world.

God gave the sun a tent.
It goes forth like a bridegroom from its retreat;
it runs its course like an enthusiastic warrior.

It goes forth from one edge of the heavens;
it returns to the other.

It never forsakes its tent.

The Law of Yahweh is perfect,
it refreshes my spirit.

The Decree of Yahweh is steadfast,
it enlightens my mind with wisdom.

The Precepts of Yahweh are straightforward,
they give joy to my heart.

The Command of Yahweh is radiant,
it gives light to my eyes.

The Edict of Yahweh is unsullied,
it lasts forever.

The Judgments of Yahweh are true,
they are just in every way.

These are more precious to me than gold,
than fine gold in abundance;

These are more sweet to me than honey,
than honey oozing from the comb.

Your servant is enlightened by your judgments,
in observing them I find a great reward.

Who can understand my mistakes?
From my failures cleanse me,
especially from those of presumption protect me
lest they gain the upper hand over me.

Then I shall not be found guilty,
I shall be free of great crimes.

May the words coming forth from my mouth
be according to your will,
the thoughts in my heart
only what you want.

O Yahweh, my Mountain and my Redeemer.

At these words, I am immediately outside, walking across the hills in the clear, clean air of the Ozarks, filled with wonder at the starry spectacle that calls to me so powerfully and fills me with a holy awe and a deep joy. The Milky Way; the mythological figures of Orion and the like; the dippers and the pole star, the carpet of stars that lead across the heavens...it is all too much to take in. And he, the Creator, calls each star by name, for he has formed each one by his Word. My being cannot but respond to this proclamation. I want to be one with creation as it gives glory to such a God.

This Psalm appears to be two poems. The first part seems inspired by Canaanite hymns of praise to the sun judged as contemporary with this Psalm. The second, another hymn of praise, touches on something central to a Jewish outlook, God's great gift to his Chosen People: the Torah, or, as the earlier tradition would say, "the Law." Despite the poem's two parts, the terms used to praise the Law make it clear that this Psalm is indeed the work of one author who is inviting us to find the Divine in both God's wondrous creation and in God's Revelation to his People.

In this Psalm, parallelism is very present and very rich. The Worker is in his work, the Artist in his art. Here the Divine can be seen and heard, experienced at a level deeper than words and concepts. This is poetry *par excellence* and a call to the faithful to use their poetic imagination.

The "Word" of Creation

Day pours forth its speech to day,
night shares its knowing with night

Without speech and without words,
without their voice being heard.

Their cry goes forth through all the earth
and their words to the end of the world.

What powerful imagery we have in the words "pours forth its speech." Creation, seen in the clear light of day, so fully and eloquently bespeaks its Creator that, like a torrent or a great waterfall, creation pours forth the sun, the clouds, the wind, the mountains, the plains, the sea.... The whole of this wonderful creation, every least little facet of it—those wonderful hidden realities that we are beginning to perceive only in our times: the sub-atomic world, DNA, the synapses of the human brain—all of creation sings to everyone who has ears to hear (even if only ears of the heart), or eyes to see. There is no place on this earth not gifted with these shining "words."

The revelation celebrated by the Psalm does not end with the setting of the sun. Night opens for us even more mysterious revelations: stars, nebulae, billions of galaxies, black holes—all sacraments of a knowledge beyond our sense-perception and conceptual grasping, a knowledge that can find its place in us only through the brilliant darkness of contemplative prayer. It is in this prayer that we enter a silence—without speech, without words, without voice—that leads us into the deepest and fullest knowledge of our God and our God's wondrous creation, which includes ourselves.

> **God gave the sun a tent.**
> **It goes forth like a bridegroom from its retreat;**
> **it runs its course like an enthusiastic warrior.**
>
> **It goes forth from one edge of the heavens;**
> **it returns to the other.**
> **It never forsakes its tent.**

Yes, the sun "tents" each night, hiding from our view. But each morning we count on a benign Providence to open the flap of that tent and to allow the radiance of the sun to shine forth.

In this context, the greatest of all days for the Jewish man was the day of his wedding. The whole village or community celebrated with him, often in a festival of light taking place at sundown. It was the young man's hour of triumph. Having won his bride, he was ready to father sons and daughters, to produce progeny before declining toward the beautiful sunset of an honored old age. The coming forth of the bridegroom to his wedding was a moment of unforgettable radiance. In the strength of that moment there was little doubt that he could meet and overcome all the challenges and obstacles of life. Like a warrior he was girded with strength, enthusiastic to go forward and to create a wonderful life with his family that would endure for generations.

For us Christians, the Christological import is obvious. The "sun," the true light that enlightens everyone who comes into this world, is the "Son." He is the Word, the bridegroom of the Church. He is the great warrior who overcomes our great enemies of sin and death. He comes forth from the Father and returns to the Father. Although his tenting is beyond the heavens, he has spoken to us in Revelation itself and in the fullest revelation: the Incarnation. This Word is, indeed, the "Law"—decree, precept, command, edict, judgment—of life, of love, of fullest meaning.

The "Word" of the Law

What words can express the experience of the Word? The poet reaches for every word in his vocabulary, and yet contents himself with four verses:

The Law of Yahweh is perfect,
it refreshes my spirit.

The Decree of Yahweh is steadfast,
it enlightens my mind with wisdom.

The Precepts of Yahweh are straightforward,
they give joy to my heart.

The Command of Yahweh is radiant,
it gives light to my eyes.

The Edict of Yahweh is unsullied,
it lasts forever.

The Judgments of Yahweh are true,
they are just in every way.

As we move into this second part of the poem, we are struck by all the different names the inspired writer gives to the "Law": decree, precepts, command, edict, judgments. Each brings its own set of images with the emotional responses they evoke. My own images might be expressed rather summarily like this:

❖ A *law*—something on the books, which I observe so as to avoid being penalized for violating it. There is a certain servile fear here.

❖ A *decree*—I think of the decree that went forth and sent Mary and Joseph to Bethlehem, an almighty pronouncement from an almighty ruler. I might not like decrees from on high, but I respect their authority with perhaps a fearful subservience.

❖ A *precept*—this evokes the image of a teacher laying down requirements for his or her class. I *might* have the wisdom to perceive that following such precepts is truly for my benefit.

❖ A *command*—here the drill sergeant appears, barking out his orders.

❖ An *edict*—a regal pronouncement, solemnly proclaimed.

❖ A *judgment*—standing in a court of law, I hear the bench setting forth its determinations.

Responding to the Law

As the images arise, each produces its own emotions. Having been stopped on the highway and ticketed, I might have a certain emotional reaction to laws. Decrees and edicts might not raise any strong feelings for me if they have not been part of my life experience. But precepts and commands may evoke painful incidents from school or military service. Depending on the circumstance, judgements could either cause me to feel like celebrating or leave me cringing.

It can be valuable to allow all of these feelings to surface and to see how they might be affecting our relationship with the Lord and "his just decrees." But whatever our reactions, we are not meant to deal only with the emotions that flow from our own particular life experiences. As we pray this Psalm-poem, we are invited to enter the inspired poet's experience of "the Law." What is this experience? He finds the Law perfect, refreshing, steadfast, wise, straightforward, a source of joy. He describes the Law as radiant, enlightening, unsullied, eternal, true and just, more precious than fine gold, and sweeter than honey. All of this can challenge us to rise to a higher level. Just what has the "Law" of God really meant in my life? Some people cower before a fearsome image of God. For others, the Law has been an overwhelming, ever-growing experience of love.

For one not familiar with the Jewish spirit, the Psalmist's exuberance regarding the Law might seem to be a flight of poetic exaggeration. But there comes to my mind a luncheon with a delightful and learned Rabbi who startled me with the statement: "What Jesus is to you, the Torah is to us." Reflecting on this statement, I understood its truth more and more. The renewed appreciation of Christians for the Presence of God in the Scriptures— texts which we do not hesitate to speak of as the Word of God, another created expression of the Word in our midst—opens us to the poet's vision in this hymn. The Psalmist invites us to cultivate such an appreciation of the divine gift of the Law so that his sentiments will clothe our own attitude toward the Precepts of the Lord, evoking the same rich emotional attendants in us.

> These are more precious to me than gold,
> than fine gold in abundance;

> These are more sweet to me than honey,
> than honey oozing from the comb.

What does gold, fine gold say to us? And honey? Rich imagery here for prayer. What did gold mean at the time God told Moses to fashion the Temple vessels and furnishings of finest gold, even while God's unfaithful People were making a golden calf? What meaning did the Magi's gold have as they laid it at the incarnate God's feet? And what does it mean in our own times? What is honey, to us today and to our forebears? So many thoughts, so many images, and so many feelings! In their turn, these will mold the way we respond to the Law and how it will enrich our lives.

The Word Forms Us

> Your servant is enlightened by your judgments,
> in observing them I find a great reward.

> Who can understand my mistakes?
> From my failures cleanse me,

especially from those of presumption protect me
lest they gain the upper hand over me.

Then I shall not be found guilty,
I shall be free of great crimes.

May the words coming forth from my mouth
be according to your will,
the thoughts in my heart
only what you want.

O Yahweh, my Mountain and my Redeemer.

It is in these verses that the poet brings together the two previous and rather distinct parts of this poem. It is because the Law is the radiance of that Sun which comes forth from the Divine—whom we Christians know to be *the Son*—that it so enlightens. It shines upon us especially in every inspired word of Sacred Scripture, written for our instruction.

Here the poet has returned to himself. How is he personally affected by the light of the Divine Precepts? We might ask ourselves if we truly pray this Psalm? Can we make these sentiments our own? Herein lies the formative role of Psalmody.

Your servant is enlightened by your judgments,
in observing them I find a great reward.

We have in the Psalm's concluding verses perfect parallelism, verse after verse. The first is a parallel of progression: the Judgments of the Lord enlighten us. When we use this God-given insight into reality to guide our actions, we will be rewarded, not so much by some future outpouring of Divine largess as by the fuller, richer, and happier life we will live right now. A life illumined by Revelation has the potential to become an exceedingly happy and rich life.

> **Who can understand my mistakes?**
> **From my failures cleanse me,**
> **especially from those of presumption protect me**
> **lest they gain the upper hand over me.**
> **Then I shall not be found guilty,**
> **I shall be free of great crimes.**

The poet realizes that he has stumbled and fallen often enough. Who can really understand what has led him astray so often? Only the Divine, only Yahweh can fully understand him. And more, can cleanse him. But this good singer wants not only to be cleansed from his past aberrations. He wants also to be protected from the possible consequences that could flow from them, especially that of presumption. For a vaunting pride can not only block Divine forgiveness, but also lead to something far worse.

There is a wonderful humility here for us to learn, expressed beautifully in the last verse:

> May the words coming forth from my mouth
> be according to your will,
> the thoughts in my heart
> only what you want.

Actually, this is more than humility. It is the making of perfect love, a complete wedding of wills. It looks not only at the exterior, but seeks that inner purity of heart.

O Yahweh, my Mountain and my Redeemer.

Yes, God is a mountain, a sure and solid high place upon which to stand and to receive unimpeded all the light that comes forth from the sun. And our God, Yahweh, is our redeemer. His light, his Law, his illumination, purchases us back from all our sins and failures.

Reflecting on this Psalm, I realize the importance of being drenched in it again and again, week after week, as we celebrate the Eucharist, the Liturgy of the Hours, or follow our own rule of prayer. I want, and I need to let the Word form my mind and heart, constantly renewing these sentiments, the hope within me. Truly, I want to know with my whole being that Yahweh, my God, is my mountain and my redeemer.

CHAPTER 5

Psalm 23: Shepherded to Eternal Life

PSALM 23 [22]

Yahweh is my shepherd.
I shall lack nothing;
I shall be led, to rest in green meadows.

I will be in the dwelling of Yahweh
all the days of eternity.
He leads me beside peaceful waters
where I can find refreshment;
he guides me into lush pastures,
as befits his name.

Though I should walk in total darkness,
I will not fear anything.
You are with me, your rod and your staff,
they will lead me.

For me, you lay my table before me
in the face of my enemies;
on my head, you lavishly pour out oil.
My cup overflows.

Certainly, I will be surrounded with goodness
    and kindness
all the days of my life.
And I will be in the dwelling of Yahweh
all the days of eternity.

If I were to pass among our Christian people, asking them to quote for me a verse from the Psalms, I feel quite certain that many, perhaps nine out of ten, would quote the same verse. And what would that verse be?

The Lord is my shepherd....

How often has it been heard at bedside and graveside, a word of comfort and consolation. And yet, how many have understood the fullness of what the Psalmist says to us in this poem?

Yahweh is my shepherd.
I shall lack nothing;
I shall be led, to rest in green meadows.

The Caring Shepherd

There is little doubt as to the "soul" of this Psalm, the word that gathers up all that the poet wants to celebrate. Nor is it surprising that a song attributed to King David—and perhaps actually composed by him—should take the shepherd as its central image.

Over the years, I have watched our monastery shepherd care for our flocks. I have ranged the hills of New Zealand with wonderful caring shepherds and seen a few at work in Israel. I even worked on a ranch for a time, and got to know the sheep and cattle. Still, I do not pretend to have that inner feel for this image that a good shepherd would have. There is a bonding that occurs between these rather defenseless little animals (although at shearing time they do not seem so small and defenseless!) and the one whom they come to know and trust as their total caregiver. With a good shepherd, the sheep have all that they need and want: "I shall lack nothing."

It is ironic that by the time our Good Shepherd arrived upon the scene and invited shepherds to celebrate his birth among us, they had become for the most part despised outcasts in Israel. When David penned those lines some ten centuries earlier, the shepherd may not have been held in highest honor, but a shepherd could become king!

Perhaps what is missed by most in this Psalm is the fullness of what is promised here. When the first verse of the Psalm is heard as an inclusion with its last verse, the promise of this Psalm is more easily heard. What is promised in the first verse, and that to which all the shepherd's care is to lead, is the restfulness of the green pastures of the last verse, a poetic image for the beatitude of the life to come, and something already to be savored in the restfulness of contemplative prayer:

I will be in the dwelling of Yahweh
all the days of eternity.

The aspiration for eternal happiness, written deep in the human heart, was not unknown to the sacred poet or to the people of his time. Their confidence in their Shepherd, the One who shepherded them through the Red Sea and across the desert into a Promised Land, was such that they knew he would yet shepherd them into eternal happiness and rest. To expect less from Yahweh would have been to set out on the course of a feverish quest for some other illusory source of satisfaction. "Our hearts are made for you, O Lord, and they will not rest until they rest in you," prayed Augustine, who knew this from experience.

A Promise of Refreshment

Green is a restful color. Spread across a meadow, it means more than rest. Green means nourishment, savor, softness, comfort, and an assurance that all will be well. Those who have rested in the divine embrace of contemplative prayer know that all this will be found whenever they return to that prayer. And they know that they will return there only when they are led by their Good Shepherd and his Holy Spirit.

The inclusion—the Psalm verses found between the promises of contemplative restfulness in the first verse and the eternal mansions of the Lord in the last verse—proclaims the loving care of the Shepherd that we can count on along our way.

> **He leads me beside peaceful waters**
> **where I can find refreshment;**
> **he guides me into lush pastures,**
> **as befits his name.**

As we allow this poem to open up within us, perhaps we need to rest for a bit, to walk in spirit beside calm waters and across fresh, green pastures, and to let peace and quiet pervade us. In this experience, we will come to know that our shepherd is the Good Shepherd.

Many of us have not experienced such pastoral scenes. Movies and TV can help city-bound folk to enter into these images today. But even with these, the rich image of pastoral life remains foreign to many and hardly conveys the depth it natively retains. Perhaps then the pray-er could use the image of a caring pastor, a faithful nurse, or a dedicated social worker.

Our Sure Guide

With the poet, we now come to speak directly and confidently to the Shepherd:

Though I should walk in total darkness,
I will not fear anything.
You are with me, your rod and your staff,
they will lead me.

How we grope in the dark, especially when there is not the least glimmer of light to give us some bearings. We are usually quite fearful: What might I bang in to? What lies ahead? Will I fall into a ditch, a crevice, or pit? What might come upon me? Some strange crawling thing? Or a wild animal? Or someone lying in wait? Yet, when we know we have a sure Guide, an all-seeing One, an all-powerful One who is well armed with "rod and staff," then indeed we can go forward without the least fear. We need but trust.

But our Good Shepherd is not content with little. He must keep giving:

> For me, you lay my table before me
> in the face of my enemies;
> on my head, you lavishly pour out oil.
> My cup overflows.

The poetic imagery has shifted a bit. The Good Shepherd is now a welcoming friend and ally. In the manner of the best Middle Eastern hospitality, the guest's head is anointed with scented oil, completing the welcoming ritual of a welcoming kiss and various ablutions. Supreme hospitality makes us feel really at home, as though everything in the dwelling is actually ours to use just as we like.

And in the midst of such joy, there is a surprising reference to enemies—my enemies are going to have to watch all of this. One feels the Psalmist might be thinking, "Let them grimace and burn!" Such a reaction is but a side note, perhaps meant to help us sense just how really human the inspired poet is, how easily we can relate to and even identify with him. But this is not where things end. We quickly move on to the more important image of the overflowing cup. How many biblical images this evokes! What a symbol of abundance: the cup filled to the brim and still being filled as it floods over the rim on every side.

This prepares us for the exuberant finale:

Certainly, I will be surrounded with goodness and
**   kindness**
all the days of my life.
And I will be in the dwelling of Yahweh
all the days of eternity.

"Certainly"—there is not the least doubt here. I am in the care of the Good Shepherd, I am one of his sheep. So goodness must surround me, embrace me, and hold me close—both goodness and kindness. There are no exceptions here; this is reality. When we realize this, "though I should walk in total darkness"—be it the dark night of the senses or of the spirit, be it any share in the saving cross—deep within we will know a sense of joy and peace, which are fruits of the Spirit.

It is no wonder that this has become the best known Psalm. And the more we are led into the fullness of its meaning, the more we will love it and be consoled and strengthened by it, even in our darkest hours. The Lord, Yahweh, is my Good Shepherd.

Chapter 6

Psalm 27:
Seek His Face

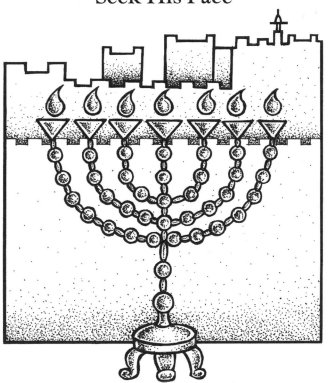

PSALM 27 [26]

Yahweh is my light and my salvation—
whom should I fear?

Yahweh is my life's stronghold—
of whom should I be afraid?

When evil ones besiege me,
seeking to devour my flesh,
it is they who stumble and fall.

Even if an army encamp against me,
my heart will not fear;
even if warriors should come against me,
I will be confident.

One thing I have asked a hundred times!
This I seek, Yahweh:
to dwell in your house

all the days of my life,
gazing upon your loveliness,
awaking each day in your Temple.

Indeed, Yahweh will treasure me in his own
    dwelling place
after the evil day;
Yahweh will shelter me in is sheltering tent,
he will find a place for me high up on
    his mountain.

Now my head is raised on high,
lifted above my foes on every side.

So I will offer in his tent
sacrifices and loud applause.

I will sing and make music for Yahweh.
Yahweh, hear my voice.
When I call, have pity and answer.

My heart says: Come, seek his face.
Yahweh, I will seek your face.
Do not turn your face from me,
do not repel your servant in anger;
be my Helper!

Do not reject me,
do not abandon me,
God, who can save me.

Even if my father and mother abandon me,
still Yahweh will receive me.

Yahweh, show me your way and lead me on the
    level path,
because of my enemies.

Do not put me into the throat of my adversaries
because false witnesses have testified against me,
    evil testifiers.

In the Victor do I trust
that I will gaze upon the beauty of Yahweh
    in the place of eternal life.

Wait for Yahweh!
Be strong! Be courageous!
And wait for Yahweh.

I am tempted to call this "William of Saint Thierry's
Psalm." Again and again this great medieval theolo-
gian and spiritual master, Bernard of Clairvaux's intimate

friend, cried out in his writings: "Seek his face! Yahweh, your face will I seek." This is undoubtedly the heart and soul of this powerful Psalm.

Yahweh Is Reassurance

Right from the poem's beginning, the sacred writer gathers reassuring images:

Yahweh is my light and my salvation—
whom should I fear?

Yahweh is my life's stronghold—
of whom should I be afraid?

Wait for Yahweh!
Be strong! Be courageous!
And wait for Yahweh.

Here is a perfect and beautiful parallelism, each of the contrasting parallels having its own common subject for parallel predicates: Yahweh—light and salvation/ stronghold; I—fear/afraid.

When all is lightsome, when we can see everything clearly, we move along peacefully and confidently. When Yahweh, the very source of all light, is our light, all fear is dispelled. We are confident that we will see all we need to see. Nothing harmful can hide to pounce upon us unawares.

Moreover, Yahweh is here to protect us, to save us from every peril. The poet invites us to take comfort in a very concrete image: a stronghold. Our imagination, fed by movies or world travel, might place us in a medieval fortress with high, stout walls and a drawbridge securely drawn up. Or life's bitter experience might place some of us in a concrete bunker or foxhole fortified with sandbags. Whatever our own image, a stronghold is a safe place against whatever our enemies may plan.

If a rich parallelism affirms my secure state:

...whom should I fear?
...of whom should I be afraid?

It is also used to affirm my enemies downfall:

When evil ones besiege me,
seeking to devour my flesh,
my enemies and my foes,
it is they who stumble and fall.

Here, a parallelism makes its point with a double subject "enemies and foes," and a double predicate belonging to both subjects, "stumble and fall." It contrasts "evil ones/ enemies and foes" with "seek to devour me/but they stumble and fall!" There is a wry humor here that occurs again and again in the Psalms; the tables are turned and the enemies lie flat on their faces. The image the poet uses, "to devour my flesh," though certainly graphic, is not meant to evoke cannibalism. Rather, it bespeaks the savageness of enemies who seek my total annihilation.

But with Yahweh on my side, confidence speaks out boldly:

> **Even if an army encamp against me,**
> **my heart will not fear;**
> **even if warriors should come against me,**
> **I will be confident.**

Let a whole army approach and pitch their tents opposite me. Let them attack. My heart will not fear! I will be confident! This is a magnificent, strong statement. No matter what happens, no matter who is against me or what they do, with Yahweh as my light, my salvation, and my stronghold, I will not be deterred or moved from my course. And what is that course? To attain the full satisfaction of my deepest longing in the unending, face to face vision of God.

Our Deepest Longings

Throughout history, there has been a prevailing, popular misunderstanding that the revelation of our destiny—our call to eternal happiness with God—was something that was only breaking into the consciousness of the Chosen People on the eve of Christ's coming. But relatively recent studies reveal that this was not the case. Scholars like Mitchell Dahood have shown that eternal life and the vision of God was very present in the aspirations and expectations of the Psalm poets. Even the earliest Psalms show this, many of which actually reach back to King David's time, a thousand years before Christ's coming. In Psalm 27, it is most clear.

When we are completely secure, confident of the all-embracing care of an invincible God, we can begin listening to the deeper aspirations of our heart, the depths of our own being. The Psalmist now invites us to "spiral down" to the deepest and most transcendent of our aspirations, and he addresses some of these desires.

Longing to Belong

First, he mentions the joy, the celebration, the sense of belonging that the Chosen People felt in the Meeting Place, Yahweh's Temple. How often, as we struggle with the million details and challenges of everyday life, do we long for all such preoccupations to be taken care of so that we will be free to live a quality life, one in accord with our more worthy aspirations.

One thing I have asked a hundred times!

When we are in touch with our deepest selves, there is no doubt at all about what we really want:

> This I seek, Yahweh:
> to dwell in your house
> all the days of my life,
> gazing upon your loveliness,
> awaking each day in your Temple.

Yes, what we seek is something permanent, not just one of those wonderful but swiftly passing moments that we sometimes experience. And we want it to be ours so completely that we are at home with it—home, the place where we wake up each morning.

Longing for a Gaze

The gaze the poet seeks here is not the detached gaze of an admirer of wondrous beauty. Rather it is the mutual gaze of lovers. He wants to gaze upon his Lord and perceive that his Lord is gazing back at him. And how beautifully the poet expresses this Divine gaze:

Indeed, Yahweh will treasure me....

His love will enfold me as one most precious to him. My heart is ensnared at this thought: Yahweh, God, the Almighty One, the Lord of all, will treasure a poor little one. Easily enough, in this moment, I can leave behind all my poverty, weakness, stupidity, and all my sin; I can just simply delight in this realization. God treasures me!

Much of me would like to stop right here and say no more....

Longing for a Place Apart

> Indeed, Yahweh will treasure me in his own
> > dwelling place
> after the evil day;
> Yahweh will shelter me in his sheltering tent,
> he will find a place for me high up on his mountain.

After all the ups and downs of this life I will be cared for, sheltered, raised up, and enjoy a place apart. One of the things the Christian tradition has cherished is this place apart—a secure place, an enclosure, a cloister. Indeed, the Spirit, speaking to us though the Second Vatican Council, has said that no local church, no diocese, is complete until it has a contemplative community in its midst. Within such a stronghold, individuals—whether they be permanent residents or retreating visitors—can find space to gaze upon the loveliness of Yahweh and listen to their own hearts, the deepest place within, saying: Come, seek his face.

But we do not have to be called to the cloister to enjoy such a place. Moreover, the Lord usually does not just pluck us out of our busyness so that we can delight in him. Rather, when we concretely express our desire to

meet the Lord on the mountain by "going apart" in whatever way is possible for us, the Lord lifts us "high up on his mountain." Our place apart might be a corner at home, a garden, a church, a library...wherever it is possible to retire regularly to be raised up and refreshed.

Confidence Is from Yahweh

So confident is the Psalmist that Yahweh, who surrounds him with such care in this life, will grant the deep aspirations that he finds within, that he begins to celebrate as if all these wondrous things were already his.

> **Now my head is raised on high,**
> **Lifted above my foes on every side.**
> **So I will offer in his tent**
> **sacrifices and loud applause.**
> **I will sing and make music for Yahweh.**

Yes, in confidence the Psalmist celebrates. And yet he knows, in reality, he still is in "the evil day." And so he pours forth a heartfelt prayer, one to which we can profoundly relate and make our own:

> **Yahweh, hear my voice.**
> **When I call, have pity and answer.**

These lines contain a progressive parallelism. The one subject, Yahweh, is first to hear and then to have pity and answer. But the next parallel, a causative one, is not so simple. In a way, it is the essence of the natural law. What our nature tells us, when we listen to it deeply and hear it rightly, is what we are to do, for this is clearly the will of the Creator, the Lord of nature. So the Psalmist, attending to the call of his deepest self, acts accordingly:

> My heart says: Come, seek his face.
> Yahweh, I will seek your face.

Of course, when the Psalmist says "heart," he is not referring to the physical organ. Rather, he speaks of the source of all our feelings, our emotions, our thoughts, and even of life itself—the place where we ever come forth from the creative hand of God.

A Plea for Assurance

Then, with an intricate piece of parallelism, the poet eloquently sets forth his plea, following it with the most touching line in the Psalm-poem, one filled with an awesome confidence:

> Do not turn your face from me,
> do not repel your servant in anger;
> be my Helper!

> Do not reject me,

do not abandon me,
God, who can save me.

"Turn your face/repel," parallels with the next, "reject/abandon," while "Helper" parallels with "God, who can save me." The use of parallels within a parallel allows the poet's skilled artistry to bring out this heartfelt prayer. Then he adds this most touching line:

Even if my father and mother abandon me,
still Yahweh will receive me.

Perhaps in our times these words have lost some of their power because we have become inured to the horror of fathers and mothers abandoning their children. Or perhaps they are even more meaningful because we see almost daily the horrendous effects of such abandonment. Here, the Psalmist proclaims that even if humans fail and betray their most basic human instincts, God will never fail in his caring love, for God *is* love.

The heartfelt prayer goes on:

Yahweh, show me your way and lead me on the
  level path,
because of my enemies.
Do not put me into the throat of my adversaries
because false witnesses have testified against me,
  evil testifiers.

The path, of course, is the path that leads to eternal life, to the face of God. Enemies, whoever they may be, would not want us to move forward securely to attain that goal. The Psalmist is especially aware of slanderers and detractors, those who give false witness. He graphically describes them as if they were some gigantic beasts who could swallow him alive, or at least prevent him from pursuing the Lord's way. But the Psalmist wants no one to be mistaken. His earnest prayer does not detract in the least from his wholehearted trust, to which he again clearly and powerfully gives voice:

In the Victor do I trust
that I will gaze upon the beauty of Yahweh
in the place of eternal life.

In the end, the inspired poet counsels all of us, his listeners, to do exactly what he knows he himself must do:

Wait for Yahweh!
Be strong! Be courageous!
And wait for Yahweh.

When Saint Benedict of Nursia, the venerable patriarch of Monte Cassino and Father of Western Monasticism, was nearing the end of his earthly course, he penned the last lines of the Prologue of his *Rule for Monasteries:* "Through patience we share in the Passion of

Christ." Waiting calls for patience, and we must indeed be patient with ourselves, with others, and with our God. Jesus so often compares our development to that of a seed, which needs time to germinate and grow. Courageously and with confidence in the Lord, we want to put one foot in front of the other, to walk the walk without wavering in our desire for that which our deepest self cries for: to gaze upon the face of God.

CHAPTER 7

Psalm 45:
A Royal Celebration

Psalm 45 [44]

I shall give voice to my poem, my King,
my tongue the pen of a skilled scribe.

You are the most handsome of all the sons of the
    human family,
graciousness flows from your lips because God has
    blessed you from eternity.

Gird your sword upon your side,
prevail by your splendor,
conquer by your majesty.

Ride in the cause of truth, triumphantly,
defend the poor.

Let your right arm's might, your sharpened arrows,
proclaim who you are.

The peoples will lie before you,
the King's foes will lose heart.

The eternal and everlasting God
    has enthroned you;
the scepter of your kingdom must be one of equity.

You must love justice and hate iniquity
because God, your God, has anointed you.

The oil of gladness is your garment,
myrrh, aloe and cassia are your robe.

Palaces of ivory, stringed instruments,
all rejoice you.

Daughters of the King adorn you,
the Queen at your right, in gold of Ophir.

Listen, Daughter, see, turn an ear:
forget your own people and your father's house
for the King desires your beauty.

Indeed, he is your Lord; pay homage to him.
The people of Tyre will seek your favor with gifts.

The Queen's robes are royal, indeed,
brocade and gold;
her robes come from the hands of the women
who weave with gold.

Let the maid be led into the King,
let her companions be brought in with her.
Let her be led in with joy and gladness,
let her be brought into the palace of the King.

In place of your fathers shall be your sons,
you will make them princes over all the earth.

I shall sing your name through all generations,
peoples will praise you from age to age.

An Invitation to Experience

My heart has created a song....

With these words, the inspired poet reminds us that
the Psalms, these poems so full of music and life, are things
of the heart, full of emotion and feeling. They share with
us an experience and invite us to enter into that experi-
ence. Here the poet is enthralled by the majesty, the
beauty, the grandeur of a king. But not just any king. This

is the messianic king, for us Christians, Christ the King. It is a heartfelt paean, sung not just about the King but *to* the King, and to his Queen, who is often seen as both the King's Spouse—the Church—and Mary, the archetype of the Church, the Mother of the King.

If the heart can compose, then indeed the tongue can be a pen. The words of the Psalms were written in minds and hearts, and sung on lips before they were ever put to parchment, though it has been the parchment that has brought them to us. The first verse of the Psalm unites with the last verse to form an inclusion, the first followed and the last preceded by a beautiful and rich benediction called down upon our King:

> I shall give voice to my poem, my King,
> my tongue the pen of a skilled scribe.
>
> You are the most handsome of all the sons of the
> human family,
>
> Graciousness flows from your lips because God has
> blessed you from eternity...
>
> In place of your fathers shall be your sons,
> you shall make them princes over all the earth.
>
> I shall sing your name through all generations,
> peoples will praise you from age to age.

Praise for the King

As so often happens, the inspired words and works of the Lord's servants are fruitful in ways that far surpass even their wildest dreams. Imagine the delight of this poet, now in the heavenly court, as he hears his words sung in hundreds of languages, day and night from all parts of the earth, proclaiming praise to the true King of kings. Surely, not even the poet's divinely inspired eloquence can begin adequately to praise the glory of that King. Nonetheless, he gifts us wayfarers with a worthy song for our King, the fairest of the sons of the human family. The Christian believer feels that, indeed, grace pours forth from the King's lips, for he has the words of eternal life, this Son who comes forth ever from the Father. More than a blessing, all the fullness of God dwells in him.

A heart filled with love and devotion, with deep admiration, thus begins to pour forth its praise. There is an integralness here, an incarnationalism, a physiognomy delightful to behold, that calls for a superlative: "The *most* handsome of all the sons of the human family," bespeaks a deeper beauty, a thing of grace, a special gift from God.

It is easy for the lover of Christ to apply this song of praise from its original object to Christ. Historically, we have no proof of Jesus' outward appearance, but there was undoubtedly a beauty about him that attracted people. A mere word, and those who met him left all—family, fortune, career—to follow him, to be with him.

In its historical context, the Psalm invites us to think of the wisdom that was poured upon the lips of David's son, Solomon—the whole, rich mythology surrounding Solomon's wisdom, with the fabulous visit of the Queen of Sheeba and the encounter with harlots. Still listening to the Scriptures, we realize that perhaps there was more wisdom in the father than in the son. All this invites us into deeper appreciation of the King as a wisdom teacher. How many of his stories flood our minds! Yes, graciousness is poured on his lips. And God has blessed him forever. If David was promised an everlasting throne, we Christians have seen the promise realized in his descendant, our eternal King.

The King's Majesty

The majesty of this kingship is now filled out in colorful poetic imagery. A royal figure, gloriously armored, rides forth as the great and most effective defender of all that is good. Here, moral goodness is as much an adorning strength of this king as is his military abilities. Indeed, it is his right hand, the hand of righteousness, which guides his deeds.

Gird your sword upon your side,
prevail by your splendor,
conquer by your majesty.

Ride in the cause of truth, triumphantly,
defend the poor.

Let your right arm's might, your sharpened arrows,
proclaim who you are.

The peoples will lie before you,
the King's foes will lose heart.

Clearly, it is precisely this king's commitment to and
love of righteousness that is the ground of the Divine
favor with which he is endowed. And that favor is now
richly, poetically described, a beautiful inclusion, a par-
allel within a parallel:

The eternal and everlasting God has enthroned you;
the scepter of your kingdom must be one of equity.

You must love justice and hate iniquity
because God, your God, has anointed you.

The King is anointed with oil. It is time for us to al-
low our own experience of oil, of being anointed or
perhaps massaged with oil, to flow to the surface of our
minds and hearts. It is the anointing of Baptism, of Confir-

mation, of Orders. It is the oil that strengthens limbs for a race and that soothes aching yet victorious limbs at the end of a race. It is the oil of gladness, of celebration. It is the anointing of the Holy Spirit.

And this King receives anointing above all his fellows. Indeed, the anointing that we all receive is but a participation in his. For David's humanity, in his Royal Offspring, is anointed with the very Godhead in the Incarnation.

> **The oil of gladness is your garment,**
> **myrrh, aloe, and cassia are your robe.**
>
> **Palaces of ivory, stringed instruments,**
> **all rejoice you.**
>
> **Daughters of the King adorn you,**
> **the Queen at your right, in gold of Ophir.**

Our poet now ushers us into the splendors of the royal court. All the senses are invited to enter into the experience. In Middle Eastern culture, scent features largely; yes, the robe's beauty is striking, but it is scent that stands out. The pungency of myrrh, the soothing fragrance of aloe, the delight of cassia. As we hear these words, many of us realize our cultural poverty. We have not allowed scents to speak to us. We hardly, if at all, relate any distinctive emotion to myrrh, aloe, and cassia. But for our poet they would speak powerfully, each evoking its own rich emotions. Are there scents that we can relate to and that evoke memories for us, incite our imaginations?

Stringed instruments fall more readily within our ken. Who has not been soothed, stirred, lifted up by the music of the violin? Our souls have vibrated with the deep tones of the cello. Like David's rival, Saul, I have been enthralled and quieted by the melodious harp. Ivory palaces might evoke certain emotions for some of us, but strings sing and resonate within almost all of us, calling forth perhaps many rich memories.

And then comes the greatest delight, the truest adornment, the daughters of the King and his Queen. Nothing in all creation is as beautiful as the human person. And when someone has been so graced as to participate fully in the divine life and nature, a true daughter or son of the King, the beauty reaches its highest.

We need to allow this poem to bring us into the rich and full experience of this splendid court. The poet celebrates the fabled sumptuousness of the Jewish court in its days of greatest luster. For us, it calls forth images of the heavenly court toward which we all are destined. Indeed, in some way we Christians have already entered it

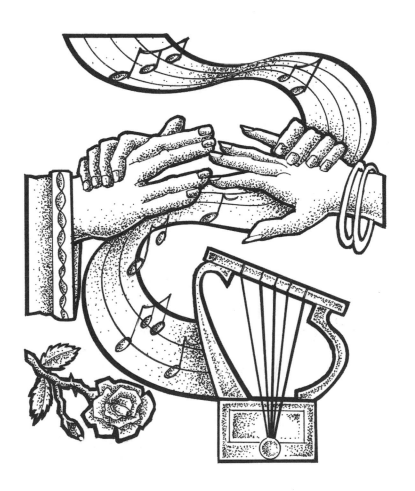

at Baptism when we entered the whole Christ, becoming one with all in his kingdom.

The Queen is a prime figure in the King's glorification as his most special and supreme adornment. Like the King, her beauty is brought out in glorious robes, joyful sounds, and beautiful companions. The Queen who held favor at court was powerful, but the poet's devotion to the King is undivided. Here too, the Queen must be seen as acknowledging the King as her Lord. Catholics readily associate the Queen with Mary, the Mother of Jesus. Today, millions from every corner of the world look to Mary, seeking her intercession while acknowledging that her power as intercessor exists only because she heeds totally the advice of the inspired poet:

> Listen, Daughter, see, turn an ear:
> forget your own people and your father's house
> for the King desires your beauty.
> Indeed, he is your Lord; pay homage to him.
> The people of Tyre will seek your favor with gifts.
>
> The Queen's robes are royal, indeed,
> brocade and gold;
> her robes come from the hands of the women
> who weave with gold.
>
> Let the maid be led into the King,

> let her companions be brought in with her.
> Let her be led in with joy and gladness,
> let her be brought into the palace of the King.

Attachment to the King

David, like the kings of his times, gathered many wives from many places. One after another held his favor. It was essential for each wife to leave behind her own place and customs and, more deeply, her attachments, so that she could truly be one with her king, wholly his. Those called to intimacy with the King must forget everything—not by some memory lapse or fading, but by relinquishing all attachments—so that they can freely give themselves totally to their King.

> **In place of your fathers shall be your sons,**
> **you will make them princes over all the earth.**

Here we have a most striking statement. The Jewish People are a people acutely aware of their ancestry. Their God is the God of Abraham, Isaac, and Jacob. Their historical accounts are full of genealogies. One's origin is very important to this People. But our inspired singer, in his devotion and in his prophetic spirit, hails a King so important, so exalted, that the King's ancestry no longer matters. And yet, it remains a matter of supreme importance that one be numbered among his offspring. What this enthusiast ascribes to his King with inflated poetic imagery will indeed be fulfilled in the One who calls himself Son of David. This is certainly a messianic Psalm, a Psalm celebrating a fulfillment beyond all the dreams that the messianic promises evoked—the mystic marriage of God himself with his People.

Images, images, images—throughout this extraordinarily rich celebration of royalty, they assail us, summon us, bring us into an experience. But what is the "soul" of this poem, this song, this symphony? Is there one word, one phrase, or one image in this Psalm that captures or best expresses it? Perhaps this Psalm comes to its fullness in its final verse:

I shall sing your name through all generations,
peoples will praise you from age to age.

It is a rich, beautiful celebration, leading to unending praise.

Chapter 8

Psalm 107:
Let Mercy Be Thanked

Psalm 107 [106]

Thank Yahweh for he is good,
for his mercy is without end.

Let all those redeemed by Yahweh tell the story
how he redeemed them from their oppression
how he gathered them in from all lands
from the east, the west, the north,
from the seas.

Some wandered through the wilderness
theirs was a trek through the desert.
They could find no place to make a dwelling
they were hungry and thirsty, drained of life.

Then they cried out to Yahweh in their distress
and he rescued them from their troubles.

He led them along a straight path
until they reached a place of habitation.

Let those who have been saved give thanks to
   Yahweh
and make known his mercy to all.
He satisfies the throat that thirsts,
the throat that hungers he fills with good things.

Some were imprisoned in darkness and gloom,
they were weighed down with heavy iron
because they went against the commands of El,
they spurned the counsel of the Most High.

Their spirits were crushed by their hard lot.
They fell flat and there was no one to help them up.
Then they cried out to Yahweh in their distress
and he rescued them from their troubles.

He brought them out of their gloom and darkness,
he broke their irons to pieces.

Let those who have been saved give thanks to
   Yahweh

and make known his mercy to all.

He breaks to pieces the bronze doors
the irons he breaks apart.

Sick because of their rebellious ways,
afflicted because of their iniquity,
their throats closed in horror of food,
they came to the very gates of Death.

Then they cried out to Yahweh in their distress
and he rescued them from their troubles.
He sent his word to heal them,
to cure them of their boils.

Let those who have been saved give thanks to
    Yahweh
and make known his mercy to all.
Let them offer thanksgiving sacrifices,
let them recount his mercy in joyful song.

As for those who sail the sea in ships,
who trade across the waters,
they have seen what the Lord can do,
the wonders of his works in the depths.

With a word, he raised the wind,
a storm that raised the waves on high;
they were thrown up to the heavens,
they were dropped into the depths.

In their fear their voices cracked,
they staggered about like drunks.
all their skill was gone.

Then they cried out to Yahweh in their distress
and he rescued them from their troubles.
he stilled the storm to a whisper,
the roaring waves were hushed.

They were happy with the calm
and he brought them to the port they desired.

Let those who have been saved give thanks to
    Yahweh
and make known his mercy to all.
Let them praise Yahweh in the assembly of the
    people,
let them praise him in the gathering of the elders.

He changed rivers into waterless gullies,

springs into parched ground,
fruitful land into salt flats
because of the wickedness of the inhabitants.

He changed the waterless gullies into pools of water
the parched ground into springs.
He brought the hungry there
he gave them a town to call their own.
They sowed fields and planted vineyards,
they harvested an abundant crop.

He blessed them, they multiplied.
Even their cattle increased.

When they are diminished and brought down
by oppression, troubles, and sorrow,
he looks with disdain on the lordly ones
and sends them to wander in trackless wastes.

He gave the poor a secure home
he made their clans his own flocks.

Let the upright see and rejoice
and all the wicked shut up!

Whoever is wise will heed these things,
will consider the mercies of Yahweh.

Our Need for Redemption

The first words of Psalm 107 express the theme or "soul" of this powerful Psalm:

Thank Yahweh for he is good,
for his mercy is without end.

The Psalmist makes it immediately clear to whom he addresses his exhortation: those who have known trouble and have been saved by the Lord. Haven't all of us known trouble and yearned to be saved? With prophetic insight the inspired writer sees redemption as universal, presaged by the redeeming of Israel from all directions: from Egypt to the south, Babylon to the east, Philistia to the west, and from all the perils of the sea.

Let all those redeemed by Yahweh tell the story
how he redeemed them from their oppression
how he gathered them in from all lands
from the east, the west, the north,
from the seas.

In this beautifully constructed poem, the author—each time underlining it with a well-colored image we can all relate to—repeats his word again and again:

Let those who have been saved give thanks to
Yahweh
and make known his mercy to all.

It is for us who have received mercy, to acknowledge the source of our redemption with thanksgiving and to proclaim the mercy of the Lord. Within a series of vignettes, again underscored by repetition, the poet weaves his secondary message: in our need, we must cry out to the Lord.

Desert Times

Then they cried out to Yahweh in their distress
and he rescued them from their troubles.

This Psalm is a lesson in prayer.

In the first vignette, the poet takes us into a region of emptiness, the desert. The immediate reference for the people of God was the Exodus, the forty years in the desert. In a desert, there are no habitations, no friends or allies, no means to dwell in a dignified way. There is nothing to feed body or soul; all is parched. Not only is the body stressed, but the spirit also knows a terrible depression. Every person journeying through this life knows times of "desert," of dryness, of loneliness, and of a sense of exile.

> Some wandered through the wilderness
> theirs was a trek through the desert.
>
> They could find no place to make a dwelling
> they were hungry and thirsty, drained of life.
>
> Out of these depths, a cry to the Lord arises.
> > And deliverance comes.
>
> He led them along a straight path
> until they reached a place of habitation…
>
> He satisfies the throat that thirsts,
> the throat that hungers he fills with good things.

(Might we not hear, as an overtone, something of the young virgin's *Magnificat?*)

Imprisonment

Perhaps the images of the Exodus bring to mind the imprisonment of Joseph, so much a part of that deliverance story. But our poet has a much wider perspective. Literal imprisonment is but an image for all the ways we are imprisoned, including the imprisonment of our own sin and folly. The poem's prison images are graphic and powerful.

> Some were imprisoned in darkness and gloom,
> they were weighed down with heavy iron

> because they went against the commands of El,
> they spurned the counsel of the Most High.

> Their spirits were crushed by their hard lot.
> They fell flat and there was no one to help them up.

And these prison images—the darkness, the gloom, the leg irons, the bronze doors of the prison—linger even as liberation occurs:

> He brought them out of their gloom and darkness,
> he broke their irons to pieces.
> He breaks to pieces the bronze doors
> the irons he breaks apart.

Illness

Then, without delay the poet hurries us into another experience of misery and liberation, the more common prison of extreme illness. And again he emphasizes that all this misery is ultimately due to sin:

> Sick because of their rebellious ways,
> afflicted because of their iniquity,
> their throats closed in horror of food,
> they came to the very gates of Death.

Again, a cry for relief, for salvation, brings immediate redemption:

He sent his word to heal them,
to cure them of their boils.

"Boils" returns our imagination to Egypt, where they afflicted the hard of heart. But it also brings us to the innocent Job who suffered, because of sin, the arrogant pride of the Evil One. It is the Word who is sent to heal Job. Only a later revelation will open this prophetic word to show its astounding fullness.

Perhaps it is because this particular affliction is so apt to be the personal experience of his listeners, the Psalmist here does not content himself simply with his recurring thematic exhortation, "let them give thanks." He gives more precise direction: thanks is to be in the form of sacrifices, the proclamation of Yahweh's mercy is to be in the form of joyful song:

Let those who have been saved give thanks to
Yahweh
and make known his mercy to all.
Let them offer thanksgiving sacrifices,
let them recount his mercy in joyful song.

Deliverance from All Harm

Again, for one last time, the poet leads us into an experience of dread and deliverance, this being perhaps the most dramatic. Although few would have actually experienced the dread of the sea, popular imagination would have supplied enough images. The scene releases the poetic imagination, first the beauty and wonder of the vast sea:

As for those who sail the sea in ships,
who trade across the waters,
they have seen what the Lord can do,
the wonders of his works in the depths.

And then the sea's savageness:

With a word he raised the wind,
a storm that raised the waves on high;
they were thrown up to the heavens,
they were dropped into the depths.

In their fear their voices cracked,
they staggered about like drunks.
All their skill was gone.

Again, the People cried to the Lord. And again, his response brings to our minds the Man from Nazareth, sailing upon his own Sea of Galilee:

He stilled the storm to a whisper,
the roaring waves were hushed.

> They were happy with the calm
> and he brought them to the port they desired.

Yes, if we turn to the Lord in our need, he will bring us to the port we desire; he will bring us safely home. The poet also has a special exhortation for sailors arriving home after such an experience:

> Let them praise Yahweh in the assembly of the
>   people,
> let them praise him in the gathering of the elders.

Now the fourfold meditation is complete. If we have lived through these experiences, we are ready for the words of the wise one. For this Psalm becomes a wisdom song, with a dramatic contrast between the wicked and those who follow Yahweh.

For the wicked, there are consequences. Their rivers and springs will dry up, their land will become salt flats. Diminishment and exile is all that lies ahead for them:

> He changed rivers into waterless gullies,
> springs into parched ground,
> fruitful land into salt flats
> because of the wickedness of the inhabitants....
>
> When they are diminished and brought down
> by oppression, troubles and sorrow,

he looks with disdain on the lordly ones
and sends them to wander in trackless wastes.

It is not so with the others. However, the others here
are not "the good." Rather, as in the Beatitudes of the
Lord Jesus and in the *Magnificat* of his mother, the others
are the poor and the hungry:

> He changed the waterless gullies into pools of water
> the parched ground into springs.

> He brought the hungry there
> he gave them a town to call their own.

> They sowed fields and planted vineyards,
> they harvested an abundant crop.

> He blessed them, they multiplied.
> Even their cattle increased....

> He gave the poor a secure home
> he made their clans his own flocks.
> Let the upright see and rejoice
> and all the wicked shut up!

His Mercy Knows No End

The epilogue of this magnificent poem brings us back
both to the prologue of the whole Psalter, to the wisdom

of Psalm 1, and forward to an even greater wisdom, the paradoxical blessings of poverty and hunger—poverty of spirit and hunger for justice sake—proclaimed on the Mount of the Beatitudes.

Whoever is wise will heed these things,
will consider the mercies of Yahweh.

And then they will *"Thank Yahweh for he is good, for his mercy is without end."*

After spending time with a Psalm like this, it is difficult to find words to express adequately the sense of the depth of this poetry's beauty and power. This is a poem that whips us about with the richness of its imagery. Too much seems to be packed into too few lines, leaving us breathless. In the end, we are happy that our ship is eventually brought peacefully to port.

The mercies of the Lord are great indeed, and we are grateful. But words, songs, even great poetry are not adequate. Rather than proclaiming the mercies of the Lord in the assembly or in the midst of the elders as the Psalm directs, I suspect many of us are more inclined to rest deeply in the quiet of prayer, knowing some profound moments of contemplation. The silent outpouring of our whole being before the Divine Goodness seems to be our call here. Saint John Cassian tells us that in ancient Egypt, after a soloist had sung or recited a Psalm, all the assembly prostrated themselves at full length and remained in silent prayer.

So, enough has been said. Now it is time for silence—silent praise and thanksgiving.

Chapter 9

Psalm 130: Out of the Depths

PSALM 130 [129]

Out of the depths I cry to you, Yahweh.
Lord, hear my voice.

Let your ears be attentive
to my cry for mercy.

If you should record iniquities, Yahweh,
Lord, who can stand?

But with you is forgiveness
that you might be revered.

I call Yahweh, my soul calls,
for his word I am waiting.

My soul looks to the Lord
as a watchman awaiting the dawn,
as a watchman awaiting the dawn.

Wait, O Israel, for Yahweh.
Because with Yahweh there is mercy
and with him abundant redemption.

He himself will redeem Israel
from all iniquities against him.

De profundis, "Out of the depths"…you have perhaps heard the expression. In the past, this Psalm was commonly known by the first two words in the original Latin. People would often promise to pray a *De profundis* for a departed friend, or receive a penance from a confessor to pray the *De profundis* three times for the faithful departed. It was a favorite prayer for the deceased. From medieval times and even up to the time when I entered the monastery, monks would ring the monastery bell for the length of a *De profundis*. It was a prayerful measure of time. (Have you ever thought of boiling your egg for the space of ten "Our Father's"? Or perhaps even for the length of one of your favorite Psalms? Turn waiting into prayer!)

A Cry from Our Depths

There is no doubt that the soul of this Psalm lies in its opening words. It is a heartfelt cry to the Lord.

Out of the depths I cry to you, Yahweh.
Lord, hear my voice.

This cry comes from the depths. The surprisingly frequent use in the Psalms of images drawn from the perils of the sea—something hardly familiar to David—invites us to think immediately of the depths of the sea where one encounters all sorts of dangers. At the same time, the constant traditional use of this Psalm in connection with the dead invites us to think of the depths of the earth, the abode of those who have gone down into death, into the grave.

However, I think we can also experience this Psalm-poem as inviting us to enter into the depths of our own being. There it is possible to encounter a terrible darkness and desolation and need. We might even think of the "dark night" so powerfully described by the mystics. In general, however, we should be slow to ascribe our darkness to some mystical state, since inner darkness can arise for so many reasons. Only if we have been faithful in using the ordinary means of Christic illumination—actively participating in the Liturgy, meeting the Lord daily in his inspired Word, faithfully giving ourselves to the practice of meditation or contemplative prayer, seeking the light that comes from a soul-friend or spiritual director, and involving ourselves in some type of active faith sharing—can we begin to explore the possibility that the darkness we encounter in our depths may indeed be part of God's activity within, by which we may be purified.

Whatever might be the cause of the darkness, loneliness, or emptiness we experience in our depths, this powerful prayer-poem can resonate within us. Out of our own depths, we can cry to the Lord with a voice of supplication, that same depth from which we hopefully long for the Lord to hear our voice and give ear to our cry.

Let your ears be attentive
to my cry for mercy.

The attentive ear—what a consolation when we are feeling desolate and alone. There comes to my mind the image of a benign elderly figure, a spiritual mother or father, who is attentively present, ready to hear the outpouring of an aching heart. For others the image might be of a mother or a father who really listened, or a teacher or friend. Yes, if only we had some tangible assurance that the Lord is attending to our anguish and pain and need…how consoling that would be!

The Mercy of the Lord

If you should record iniquities, Yahweh,
Lord, who can stand?

**But with you is forgiveness
that you might be revered.**

We are laden with our iniquities, our sins. And God is just. If he only operated from justice, we would be in trouble, to say the least. But Saint Bernard, in one of his beautiful sermons on the Song of Songs, reminds us that God has two feet: one of justice, the other of mercy. God's justice is real, but his mercy is above all his works.

The reason the Psalmist gives for the merciful forgiveness of the Lord might seem strange to us: "that you might be revered." Actually, the Hebrew rendition for this phrase is the word "feared," but there are different kinds of fear. Here, its use gives us to understand a reverential fear rather than a servile fear. Hence the translation, "that you might be revered." The Psalmist does not mean to impute a motive to God, but rather to express a result in us. If God did not forgive us of the crushing, deforming burden of our sin, we could hardly come to him with a reverential fear. Rather, we would be filled with the terror of the eternally lost before an all-good God who justly allows us to suffer the consequences of what we have freely chosen. But when we are in the domain of forgiveness, experiencing how our good God indeed forgives all our iniquities, we are filled with joy, peace, thanksgiving, and love, as well as a profound reverence for a power that can and does wipe away all our iniquities. Blessed be this God!

Up to this point in our poem-prayer we have been speaking to Yahweh the Lord. In the third verse, we turn to speak to others, to share what we are living.

Waiting upon the Lord

> I call Yahweh, my soul calls,
> for his word I am waiting.
>
> My soul looks to the Lord
> as a watchman awaiting the dawn,
> as a watchman awaiting the dawn.

We are calling. We are waiting—waiting with the eagerness and the sureness of a sentry who watches for the dawn and the end of his night's service. The poet believes that this image so powerfully conveys the sentiments that predominate he actually repeats the line, and thus emphasizes it. Perhaps the poet was a soldier or a night watchman in his city or village and so is speaking from personal experience. I recently spent some time at a convent in Central Africa where the nuns have suffered greatly. There is a single grave in their cemetery by the convent gate; it is that of Mother Agnes who was cut to pieces while she held off brigands, giving her nuns time to flee into the jungle. The nuns now have armed watchmen patrolling the convent walls all through the night. Seeing the watchmen night after night, I could sense their eagerness for the dawn, when they could mount their bicycles and head for home and rest.

This is so powerful an image. We might have personally experienced what the poem seeks to convey, not as a watchman, but as one keeping vigil at the bedside of a loved one, or as one awaiting the return of someone very dear. Certainly the poem conveys the weariness of one who has watched all night, but more so, the hope—a very certain hope—for the dawn always comes no matter how long the night.

For us Christians, the whole expectation of the Second Coming of Christ can find a voice here. The forgiving and healing Word we await is an infinitely loving and compassionate Person, our Incarnate God of Love. And our hope is as sure as God.

At this point the Psalmist lets escape from his throat a cry that was probably a byword of the People in exile:

Wait, O Israel, for Yahweh!

Sometimes waiting is the only thing we can do as individuals and as a people: we can only wait for the mercy of God. Think of a time of flood when the waters run high—we must wait for the rain to stop; or a time of draught with fields burning—we must wait for the rain to come. More prosaically, we sit in an airport waiting for the skies to clear so we can continue our journey.

The Lord Will Take Care

> **Wait, O Israel, for Yahweh.**
> **Because with Yahweh there is mercy**
> **and with him abundant redemption.**
>
> **He himself will redeem Israel**
> **from all iniquities against him.**

Having sounded the People's cry, the Psalmist addresses his community. Here, the richness of God's mercy is given concrete color with the image of redemption. We Christians immediately think of what is for us *the* Redemption, when our Lord and Savior "paid" the price for our sin by offering himself in sacrifice on Calvary's Hill. For our Jewish brother who wrote this poem, redemptive sacrifice was a regular part of his life. The rituals of the Covenant called for sacrifice on more than one occasion. In fact, as the Gospel according to Saint Luke tells us, Jesus, as a good Jew, was taken to the Temple in Jerusalem on the fortieth day of his life and "redeemed" by the offering of a pair of turtledoves. Moreover, the law provided for many other instances of redemption such as goods and property given in surety, from slavery or serfdom, and the like. The message for us rings true: no matter what kind of mess we get ourselves into, we can hope in the Lord Yahweh for he redeems.

The final half of this fourth verse is a strong affirmation of faith and trust, with the emphasis on the Lord. Our iniquities are committed against him; therefore, he himself will do the redeeming. Again, for Christians this will spontaneously take on an incarnational meaning. It is Yahweh himself who has come to us in the incarnation, in Christ. And because he is God, whose acts have all the worth and dignity of divine acts, Christ can pay the infinite "price" for our redemption, due because of "all our iniquities against him."

As we reflect on this Psalm-poem, we can more readily understand its popularity. It is short, easy to remember in its entirety, easy to fit into moments of prayer. Yet, it touches some of our deepest emotions. We all know darkness, we all have our fears. And it gives us what we on the journey most need: hope.

Out of the depths I cry to you, Yahweh!

CHAPTER 10

The Names of God

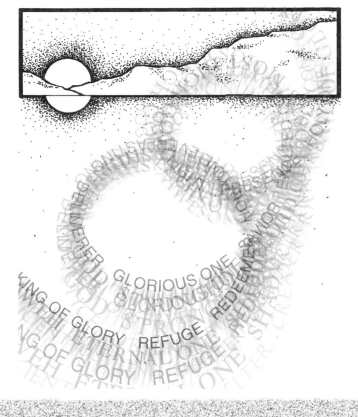

So come, Yahweh, my Lord,
work a miracle for me,
for the sake of your Name, which is truly good.

(Ps 109:21)

Dennis or Dionysius, the Areopagite—remember him? He was an Athenian who heard Paul the Apostle and went on to become a bulwark of the Church in that central city. The great Christian writers of the Middle Ages were often very humble men and women. They often did not sign their works—anonymous works (like *The Cloud of Unknowing)* that continue to nourish us today. Some went even further. In order to obtain a better reception for the wisdom they were sharing they dared to ascribe their work to some notable figure who already had a good hearing. Thus, a wise Syrian monk of the fifth century ascribed his profound classic, *The Divine Names*, to the historic Dionysius.

This work describes three kinds of contemplation. There is direct contemplation, by which one plunges immediately into the divine depths. This is the practice of Centering Prayer. There is circular contemplation, the way of one who repeatedly looks at the object being contemplated from all different angles. Little by little the beholder is drawn into a fuller and fuller sense of the Reality. And there is oblique contemplation, whereby one beholds the different works of creation and lets them lead one to their Creator. This is the path the Psalms most frequently employ to lead us into God, into true contemplation.

As we pray the Psalms one after the other and are led into deep contemplation, one after another we encounter various Names of God. Meditating on each of the holy Names and letting them call forth all their own proper imagery can open for us something of the fullness of the Psalter's poetic revelation. The Divine Names can unlock a door to the divine, and even open it. Here the poet stretches his craft to its limits in an effort to name the unnamable, to express the inexpressible, the very name of he who is.

Repeating the holy Names of God can be more powerful than any litany or mantra. Indeed, the contemplation of the Names can become a spiral leading us up into the very Center, the very Heart of God. Sometimes the Hebrew name given to God in a particular Psalm seems to sum up the whole basic message of the Psalm (for example, *Bestower* in Psalm 18:33) providing a wealth of imagery for contemplation. As we spend more time with the images these Names evoke, when we encounter the Names in the poetry itself, a richness will immediately illumine the verse or stanza within which they are set. They are as it were precious gems of many colors and facets, set in a finely wrought bracelet or tiara.

To facilitate our contemplation of these names I list them here, following the order in which one comes upon them in the Psalter, indicating in each case the place where it is first encountered.

Again, there is the challenge of translation. Certain Hebrew words obviously can be translated by more than one English equivalent. For each name found in the Hebrew text, I have tried to employ a specific English equivalent, which is probably the best we can do in working with a text in translation.

Yahweh	1:2
Enthroned	2:4
Lord	2:4
My Suzerain	3:3
My Glorious One	3:3
My God	3:7

God of my Vindication	4:2
My King	5:3
Exalted One	7:8
Most High	7:9
God the Just	7:10
Most High God	7:11
Savior	7:11
Righteous Ruler	7:12
El	7:12
Vindicator	7:12
Victor	7:13
Yahweh Most High	7:18
Stronghold for the Oppressed	9:10
King of Zion	9:12
The Lofty One	10:4
Everlasting King	10:16
Yahweh God	10:12
The King of Eternity	10:16
The Just One	11:3
Yahweh the Just	11:5
The Upright One	11:7
Eternal One	12:8
My Strength	18:2

My Rock	18:3
My Fortress	18:3
My Mountain	18:3
My Deliverer	18:3
My Stronghold	18:3
My Staff	18:9
The Strong One	18:28
My Lamp	18:29
Bestower	18:33
God of My Triumph	18:47
My Redeemer	19:15
Jacob's God	20:2
My Shepherd	23:1
The Presence of Jacob	24:6
The One of Eternity	24:7
King of Glory	24:8
My Light	27:1
My Salvation	27:1
Stronghold of my Life	27:2
My Strong Shield	28:7
My Refuge	28:8
The Holy One	29:2
The God of Glory	29:3

My Helper	54:6
Sustainer of my Life	54:6
Ransomer	55:18
Primeval One	55:20
Provider	55:23
Benefactor	55:23
Avenger El	57:3
Truly Great One	57:10
God of Hosts	59:6
God of Israel	59:6
My Triumph	62:8
My Mountain Fortress	62:8
Investigator	64:7
God of the arrow	64:8
Triumphant God	65:6
Rider of the clouds	69:5
Father of the fatherless	68:6
Defender of widows	68:6
The One of Sinai	68:9
Rider of his heavens	68:34
Most High of Israel	68:35
Mount of Succor	71:3
My Hope	71:5

Near One	119:151
Enthroned of Jerusalem	125:1
Reliable	127:2
Israel's Most High	128:6
Mighty of Jacob	132:2
Resident of Jerusalem	135:21
God of Heaven	136:26
The Lofty	138:6
My Rampart	144:3
My Fastness	144:3
My Bulwark	144:3
My Haven	144:3
Majesty	145:5
Master	145:7
Rebuilder of Jerusalem	147:2
Healer of the brokenhearted	147:3
Binder of our wounds	147:3
Supreme Maker	149:2

As we ponder these many wondrous names inspired by the Most High, we cannot help but think what a rich mine we have here for those seeking names for the Almighty, which are not gender-specific. Nonetheless, the more "impersonal" names such as these cannot be allowed to exclude the personal. A significant part of the Revelation we are privileged to share with our Jewish sisters and brothers is this: the personal revelation of our God of love.

We must admit that for us humans, and from our experience, the person is always experienced as either female or male. So our personal experience of God, as long as it remains on the human level (and our rational discourse is always on this level) is gender specific. But also, we know that our experience of God must transcend the rational, for God is beyond all that the rational mind can ever hope to embrace.

Holy and Awesome is his Name!

(Ps 111:9)

Praise Yah!

I f we ever have the courage, the grace, and the leisure to pray the entire Psalter through, when we arrive at the five "Alleluia Psalms" (numbers 146–150), which bring this wonderful collection of poems to a culminating close, these words will indeed be ours, expressing the fullness of what we have experienced. They are hymns that celebrate the power and beneficence of God, which contrasts so completely with our weakness and need. Knowing our almost total inability to respond worthily to such a God, we call upon all creation to help us, the celestial, the terrestrial, and even that beneath the earth (cf. Ps 148).

Sing to Yahweh a new song,
Yahweh's praise in the gathering of the devoted.

Let Israel rejoice in the Supreme Maker,

the children of Zion be happy in their King.

Let them praise Yahweh's name with dancing,
make music to Yahweh with tambourine and lyre.

Because Yahweh delights in Yah's people....

(Ps 149:1–4)

Let everything that breathes praise Yah!
Praise Yah!

(Ps 150:6)

Suggested Reading

Dahood, Mitchell. *The Psalms: A New Translation with Introduction and Commentary,* Anchor Bible (New York: Doubleday, 1965).

Masini, Mario. *Lectio Divina: An Ancient Prayer That Is Ever New,* tr. Edmund Lane (Staten Island: Alba House, 1998).

Merton, Thomas. *Bread in the Wilderness* (Collegeville, MN: The Liturgical Press, 1953).

Merton, Thomas. *Opening the Bible* (Collegeville, MN: The Liturgical Press, 1970).

Pennington, M. Basil. *Lectio Divina: Renewing the Ancient Practice of Praying the Scriptures* (New York: Crossroad, 1998).

Pennington, M. Basil. *William of Saint Thierry: The Way of Divine Union* (Hyde Park, NY: New City Press, 1998).

Van Deusen, Nancy. *The Place of the Psalms in the Intellectual Culture of the Middle Ages* (Albany, NY: State University of New York Press, 1999).

Father M. Basil Pennington, ocso, is a Cistercian (Trappist) monk. He joined the monastic community in 1951, and in 1968 collaborated with Thomas Merton in founding Cistercian Publications and pioneering the translation of the Cistercian Fathers into English.

In 1971, in response to Paul VI's request that the Cistercians help the Church renew its contemplative dimension of life, Father began teaching, leading retreats, and writing about the Order's ancient method of contemplative prayer, popularly known as Centering Prayer. His ministry has taken him to over fifteen countries, including China, where he has engaged in ecumenical and interreligious dialogue. His 1000 articles and over 50 books have been published in twenty-five languages.

In January 2000, Father was appointed Superior of Assumption Abbey in Ava, Missouri, and six months later was elected Abbot of Holy Spirit Abbey in Conyers, Georgia.

auline
BOOKS & MEDIA

The Daughters of St. Paul operate book and media centers at the following addresses. Visit, call or write the one nearest you today, or find us on the World Wide Web, www.pauline.org

CALIFORNIA
3908 Sepulveda Blvd., Culver City, CA 90230; 310-397-8676
5945 Balboa Ave., San Diego, CA 92111; 858-565-9181
46 Geary Street, San Francisco, CA 94108; 415-781-5180

FLORIDA
145 S.W. 107th Ave., Miami, FL 33174; 305-559-6715

HAWAII
1143 Bishop Street, Honolulu, HI 96813; 808-521-2731
Neighbor Islands call: 800-259-8463

ILLINOIS
172 North Michigan Ave., Chicago, IL 60601; 312-346-4228

LOUISIANA
4403 Veterans Memorial Blvd., Metairie, LA 70006; 504-887-7631

MASSACHUSETTS
Rte. 1, 885 Providence Hwy., Dedham, MA 02026; 781-326-5385

MISSOURI
9804 Watson Rd., St. Louis, MO 63126; 314-965-3512

NEW JERSEY
561 U.S. Route 1, Wick Plaza, Edison, NJ 08817; 732-572-1200

NEW YORK
150 East 52nd Street, New York, NY 10022; 212-754-1110
78 Fort Place, Staten Island, NY 10301; 718-447-5071

OHIO
2105 Ontario Street (at Prospect Ave.), Cleveland, OH 44115; 216-621-9427

PENNSYLVANIA
9171-A Roosevelt Blvd., Philadelphia, PA 19114; 215-676-9494

SOUTH CAROLINA
243 King Street, Charleston, SC 29401; 843-577-0175

TENNESSEE
4811 Poplar Ave., Memphis, TN 38117; 901-761-2987

TEXAS
114 Main Plaza, San Antonio, TX 78205; 210-224-8101

VIRGINIA
1025 King Street, Alexandria, VA 22314; 703-549-3806

CANADA
3022 Dufferin Street, Toronto, Ontario, Canada M6B 3T5; 416-781-9131
1155 Yonge Street, Toronto, Ontario, Canada M4T 1W2; 416-934-3440

¡También somos su fuente para libros, videos y música en español!

THE POETRY AS PRAYER SERIES

offers poetic verse as a means to prayer
exploring the connection
between culture and religion,
creativity and mysticism, literature and life.

Included in the series:

Poetry as Prayer
Denise Levertov

By Murray Bodo, OFM
Illustrated by Alan Giana
#5924-9
paperback, 144 pages

Poetry as Prayer
Thomas Merton

By Robert Waldron
Illustrated by Helen Kita
#5919-2
paperback, 200 pages

Poetry as Prayer
Jessica Powers
By Bishop Robert F. Morneau
Illustrated by Joseph Karlik
#5921-4
paperback, 176 pages

Poetry as Prayer
The Hound of Heaven
By Robert Waldron
Illustrated by Anthony Lobosco
#5914-1
paperback, 160 pages

...with more titles to follow!

To order, contact:

auline
BOOKS & MEDIA
50 Saint Pauls Avenue, Boston, MA 02130-3491
1-800-876-4463
www.pauline.org

or from the Center nearest you.

בַּחֲנֻפֵי לַעֲגֵי מָעֹוג חָרֹק עָלַי שִׁנֵּימֹו׃

אֲדֹנָי כַּמָּה תִּרְאֶה הָשִׁיבָה נַפְשִׁי מִשֹּׁאֵיהֶם מִכְּפִירִים יְחִידָתִי׃

אֹודְךָ בְּקָהָל רָב בְּעַם עָצוּם אֲהַלְלֶךָּ׃

אַל־יִשְׂמְחוּ־לִי אֹיְבַי שֶׁקֶר שֹׂנְאַי חִנָּם יִקְרְצוּ־עָיִן׃

כִּי לֹא שָׁלֹום יְדַבֵּרוּ וְעַל רִגְעֵי־אֶרֶץ דִּבְרֵי מִרְמֹות יַחֲשֹׁבוּן׃

וַיַּרְחִיבוּ עָלַי פִּיהֶם אָמְרוּ הֶאָח הֶאָח רָאֲתָה עֵינֵינוּ׃

רָאִיתָה יְהוָה אַל־תֶּחֱרַשׁ אֲדֹנָי אֲל־תִּרְחַק מִמֶּנִּי׃

הָעִירָה וְהָקִיצָה לְמִשְׁפָּטִי אֱלֹהַי וַאדֹנָי לְרִיבִי׃

שָׁפְטֵנִי כְצִדְקְךָ יְהוָה אֱלֹהָי וְאַל־יִשְׂמְחוּ־לִי׃

אַל־יֹאמְרוּ בְלִבָּם הֶאָח נַפְשֵׁנוּ אַל־יֹאמְרוּ בִּלַּעֲנוּהוּ׃

יֵבֹשׁוּ וְיַחְפְּרוּ יַחְדָּו שְׂמֵחֵי רָעָתִי

יִלְבְּשׁוּ־בֹשֶׁת וּכְלִמָּה הַמַּגְדִּילִים עָלָי׃

יָרֹנּוּ וְיִשְׂמְחוּ חֲפֵצֵי צִדְקִי וְיֹאמְרוּ תָמִיד

יִגְדַּל יְהוָה הֶחָפֵץ שְׁלֹום עַבְדֹּו׃

וּלְשֹׁונִי תֶּהְגֶּה צִדְקֶךָ כָּל־הַיֹּום תְּהִלָּתֶךָ׃

לַמְנַצֵּחַ לְעֶבֶד־יְהוָה לְדָוִד׃

נְאֻם־פֶּשַׁע לָרָשָׁע בְּקֶרֶב לִבִּי

אֵין־פַּחַד אֱלֹהִים לְנֶגֶד עֵינָיו׃

כִּי־הֶחֱלִיק אֵלָיו בְּעֵינָיו לִמְצֹא עֲוֹנֹו לִשְׂנֹא׃

דִּבְרֵי־פִיו אָוֶן וּמִרְמָה חָדַל לְהַשְׂכִּיל לְהֵיטִיב׃ [יִמְאָס׃

אָוֶן יַחְשֹׁב עַל־מִשְׁכָּבֹו יִתְיַצֵּב עַל־דֶּרֶךְ לֹא־טֹוב רָע לֹא

טֹוב׃